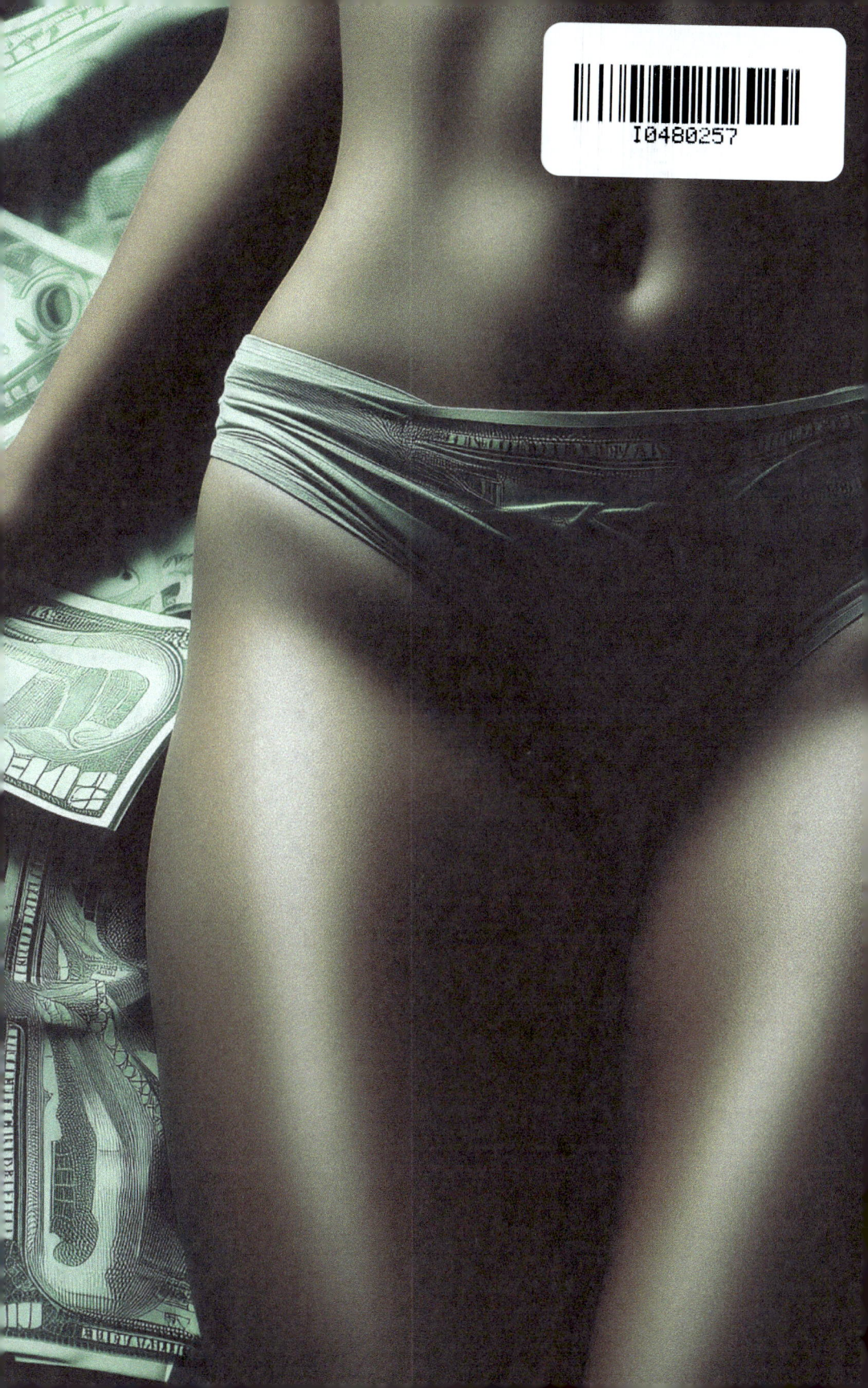

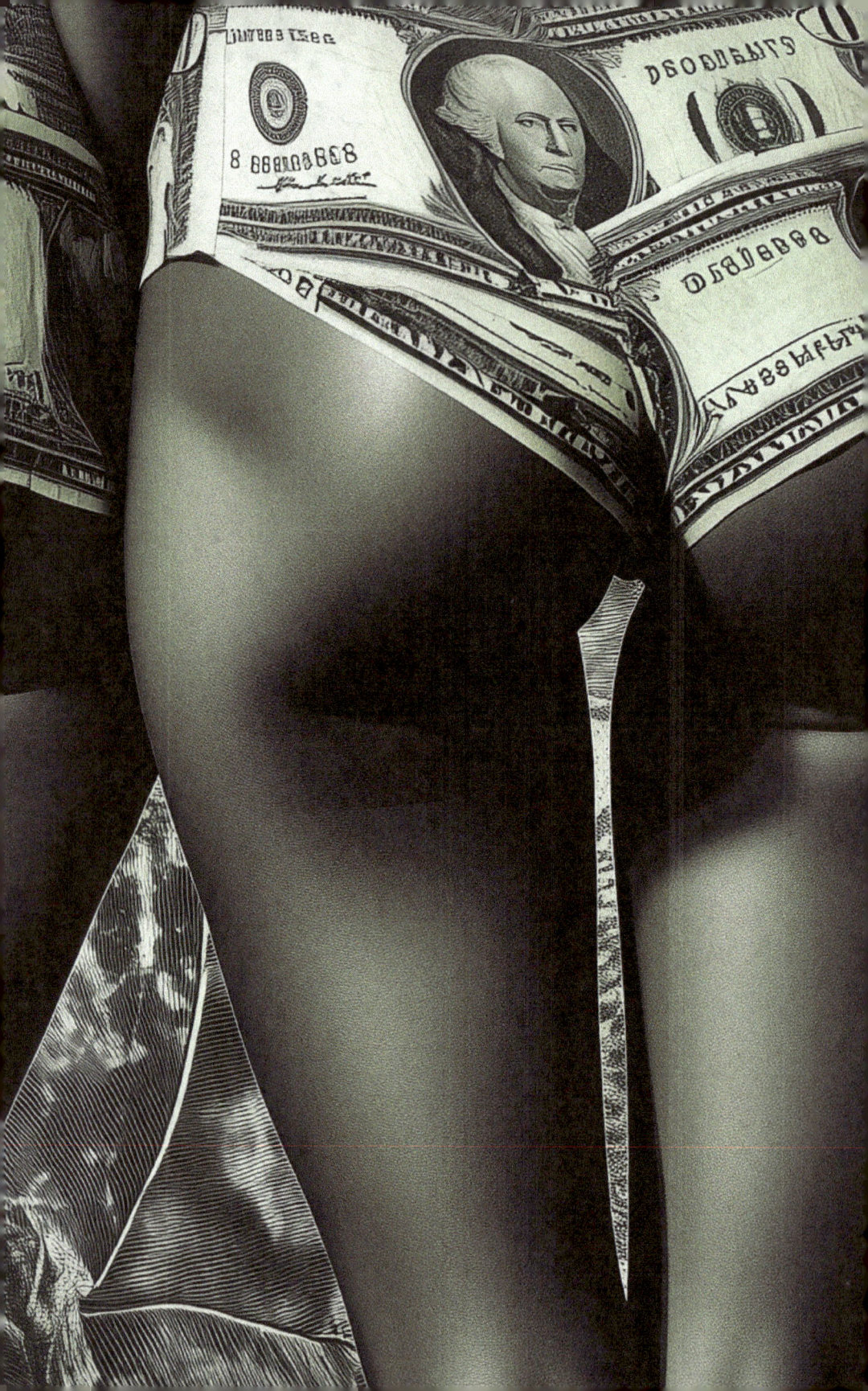

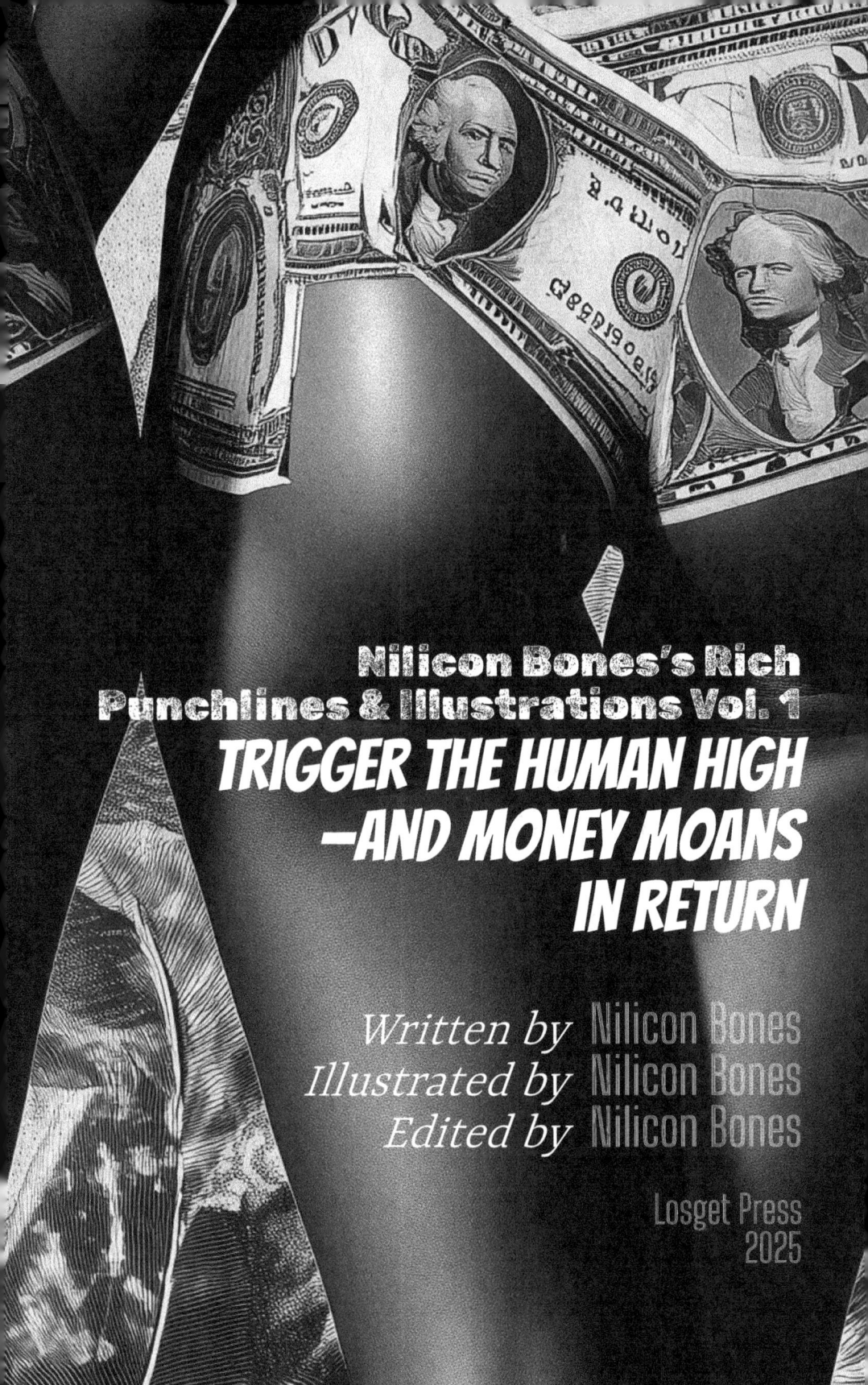

Nilicon Bones's Rich
Punchlines & Illustrations Vol. 1

TRIGGER THE HUMAN HIGH
—AND MONEY MOANS
IN RETURN

Written by Nilicon Bones
Illustrated by Nilicon Bones
Edited by Nilicon Bones

Losget Press
2025

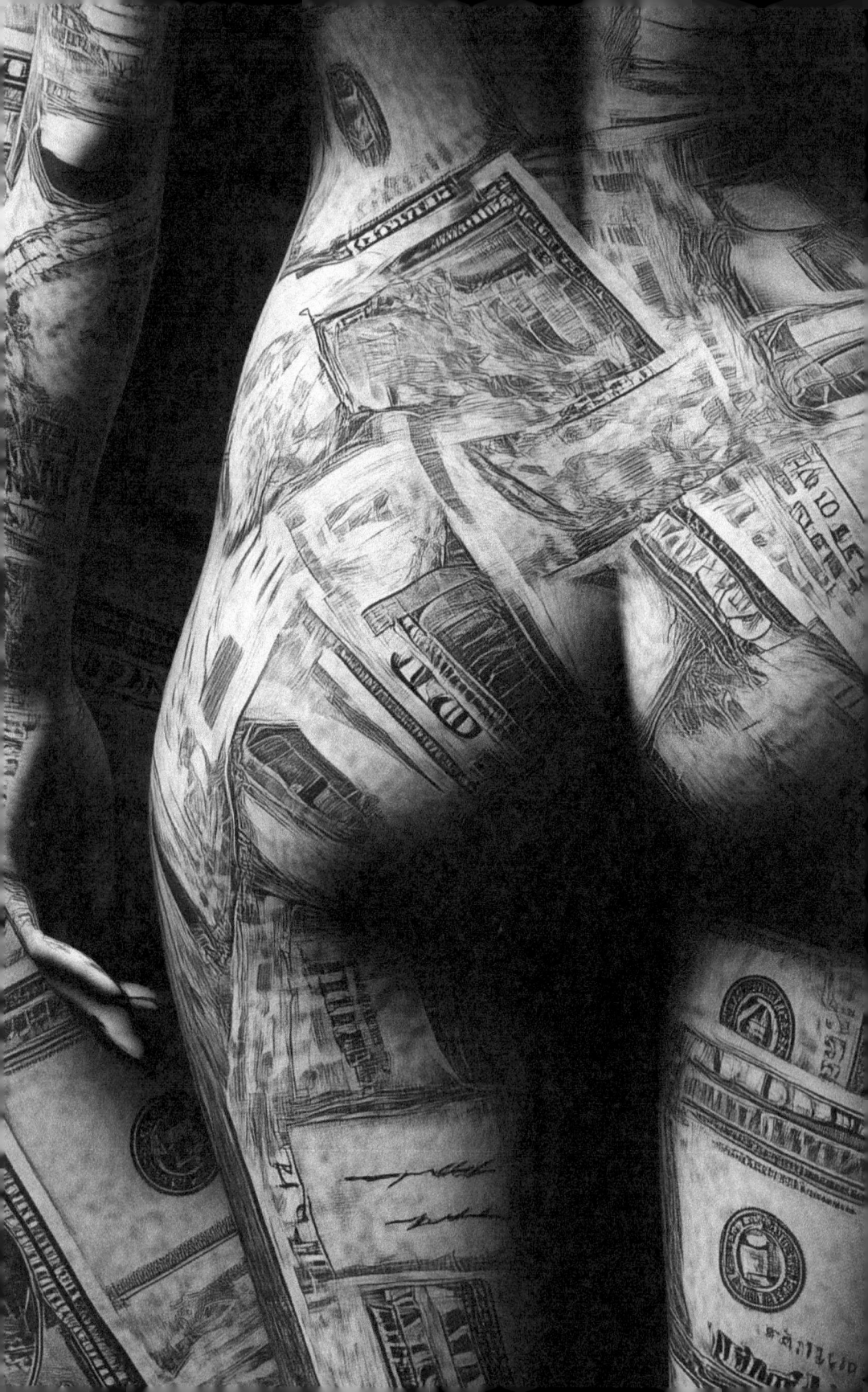

Preface

This book presents 82 fundamental rules of money—each distilled into a single punchline, and each accompanied by a sharp, editorial-style illustration.

These rules are not motivational fluff, but precision tools: clear, direct, and designed to shift the way you think about money—how to seek it, keep it, and protect it.

You won't find anecdotes or theory here. What you'll find is clarity.

Any page might contain the single idea that changes how you handle money for the rest of your life.

If you can truly understand—and remember—even one line, you may already be ahead of 99% of humanity.

LOSGET
PRESS

Published in the United States by Losget Press, Los Angeles.
Originally published in paperback in the United States by Losget Press, in 2025.
Library of Congress Cataloging-in-Publication Data
Names: Bones, Nilicon, author.
Title: *Nilicon Bones's Rich Punchlines & Illustrations Vol. 1: Trigger the Human High—And Money Moans in Return* / all texts and illustrations by the author.
Description: First edition. | Los Angeles: Losget Press, 2025.
Identifiers: LCCN 2025908706 | ISBN 978-1-951364-41-0
Subjects: LCSH: 1. Wealth—Quotations. 2. Success—Quotations. 3. Graphic satire.
Classification: LCC PN6231.W38 2025 | DDC 332.024—dc23
First printed in the United States in 2025.
E-mail: losgetpress@gmail.com

Contents

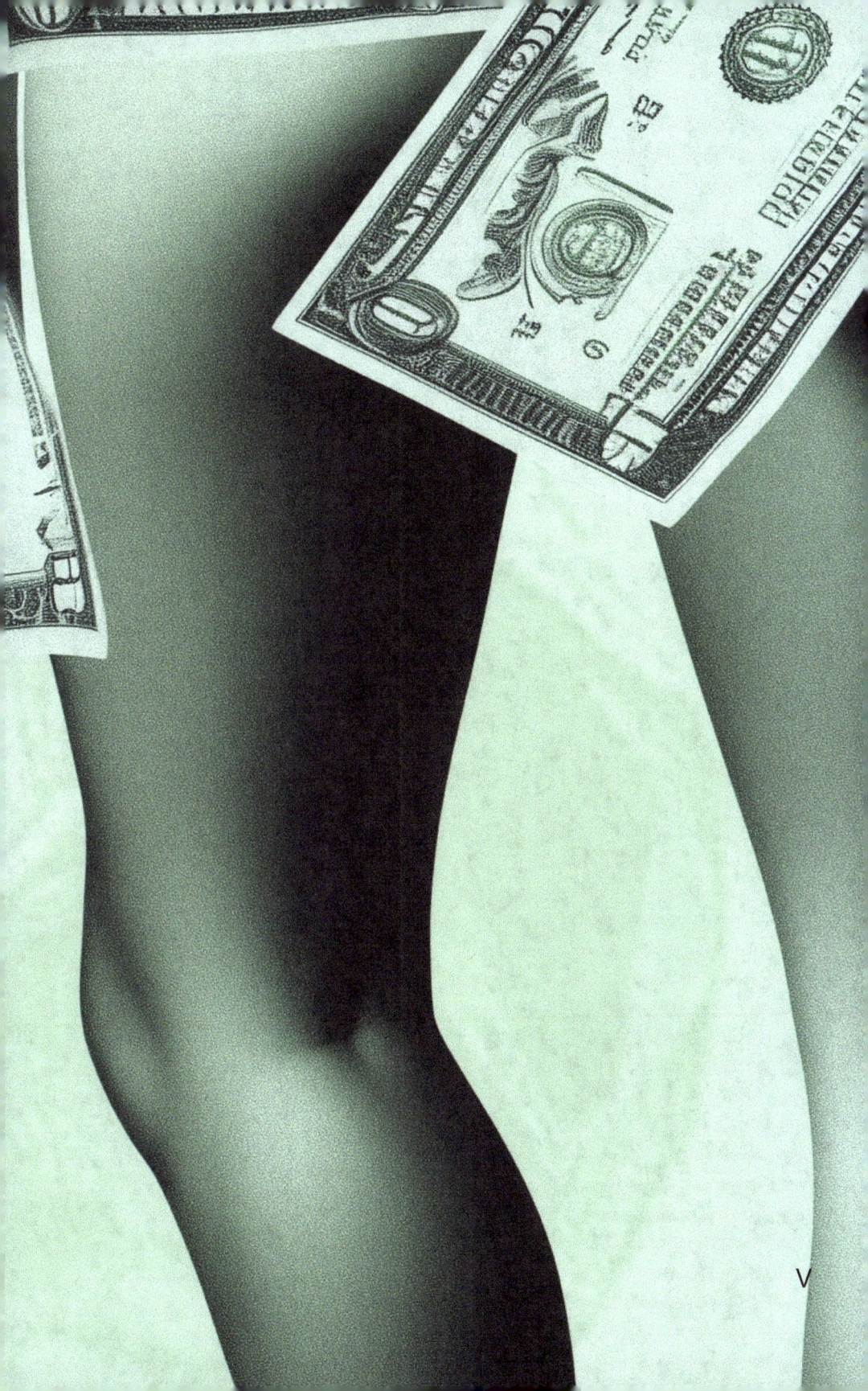

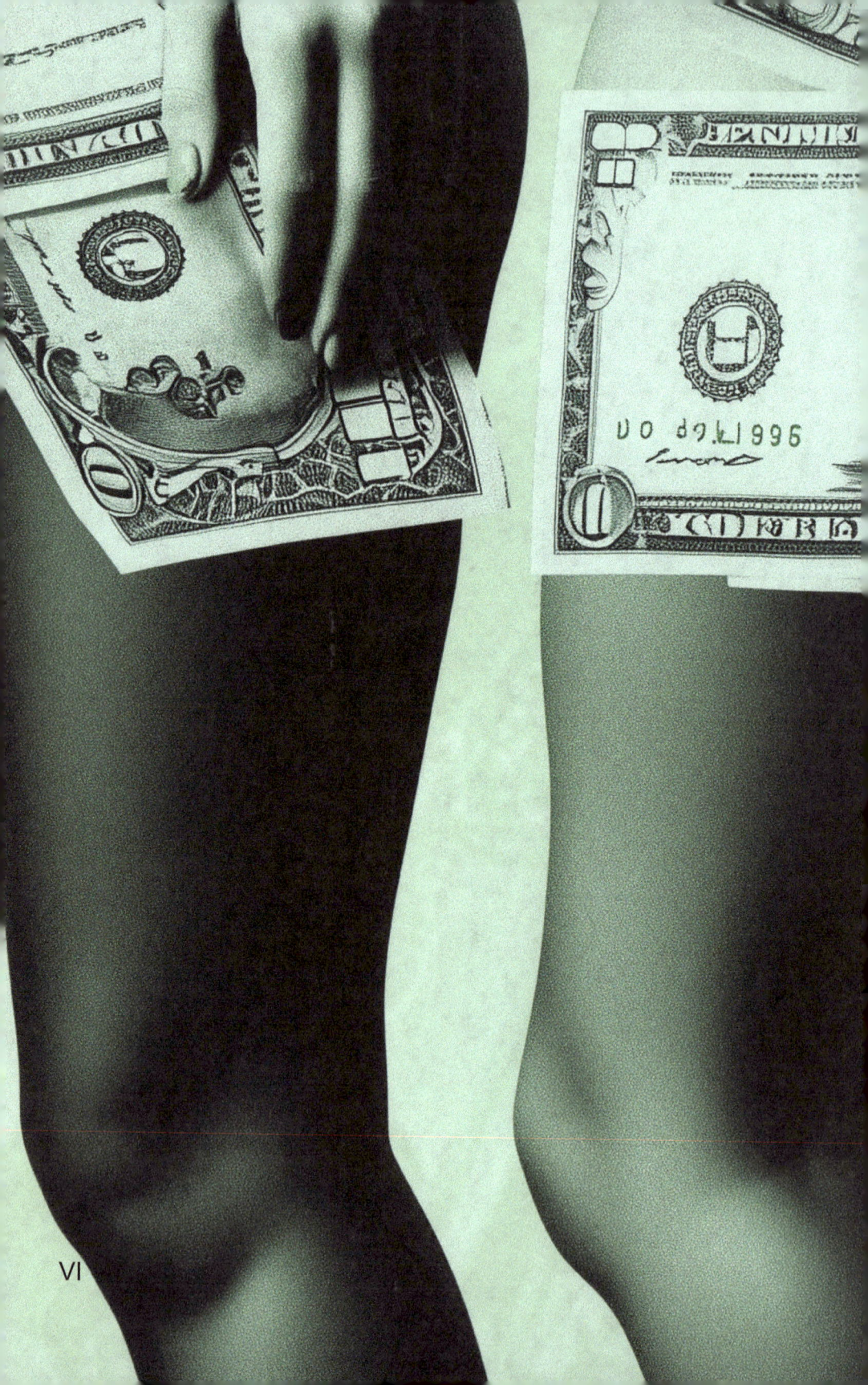

VI

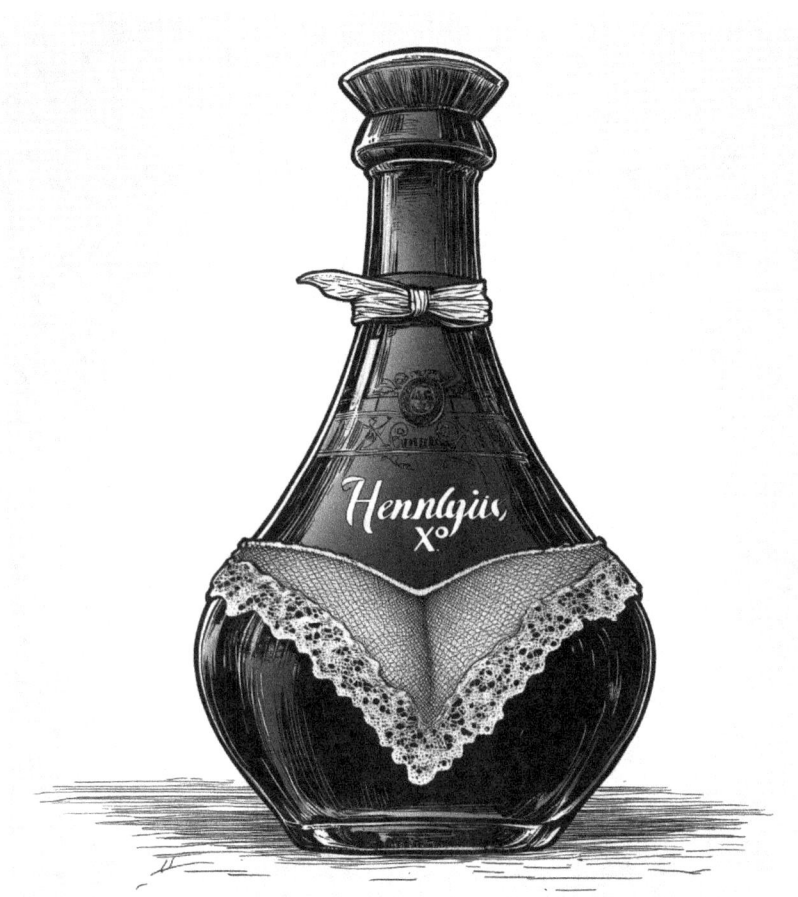

TRIGGER THE HUMAN HIGH—AND MONEY MOANS IN RETURN.

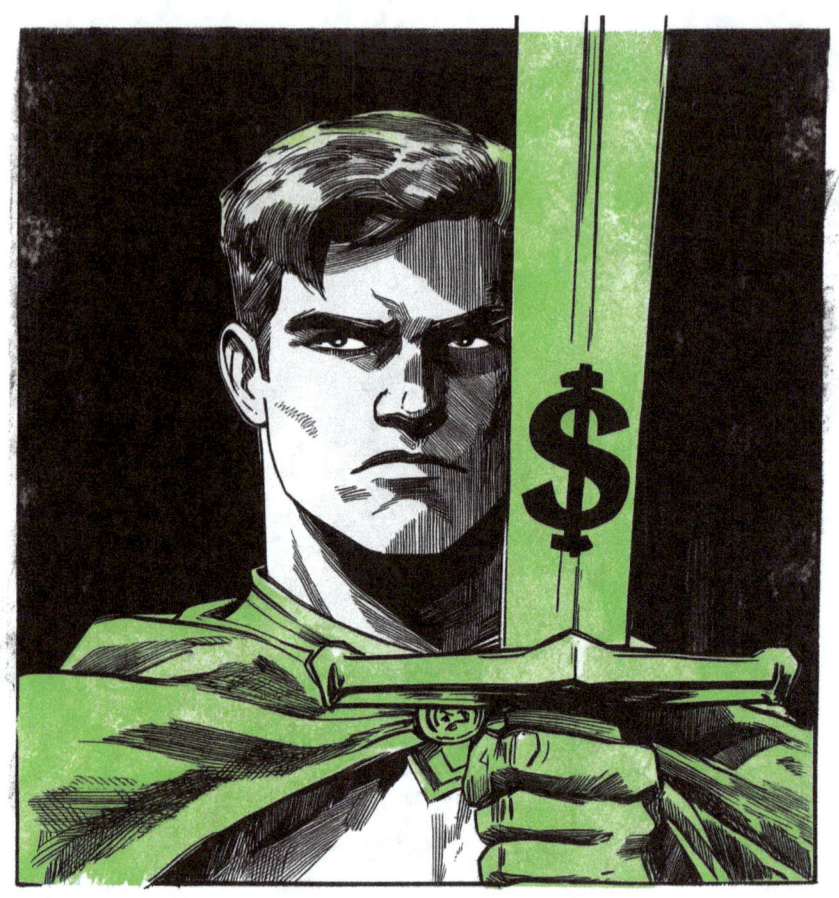

IN THIS ERA WHEN KNIGHTS ARE EXTINCT, MONEY IS A MAN'S SWORD.

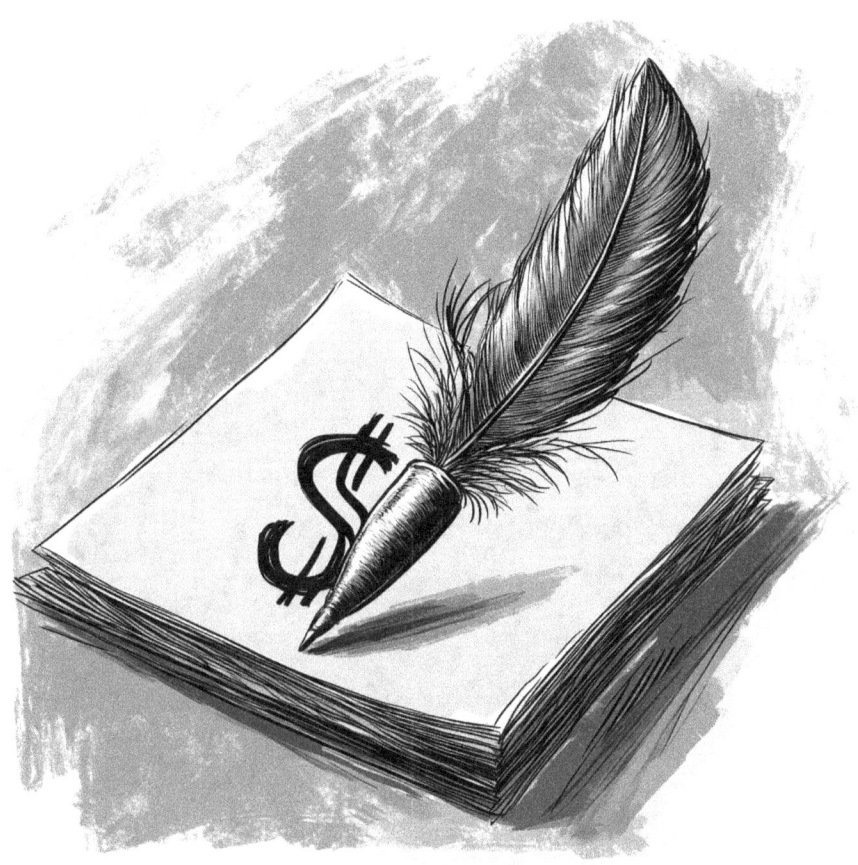

POETRY DIDN'T DIE—IT BECAME ADVERTISING; POETS DIDN'T VANISH— THEY BECAME SALESMEN.

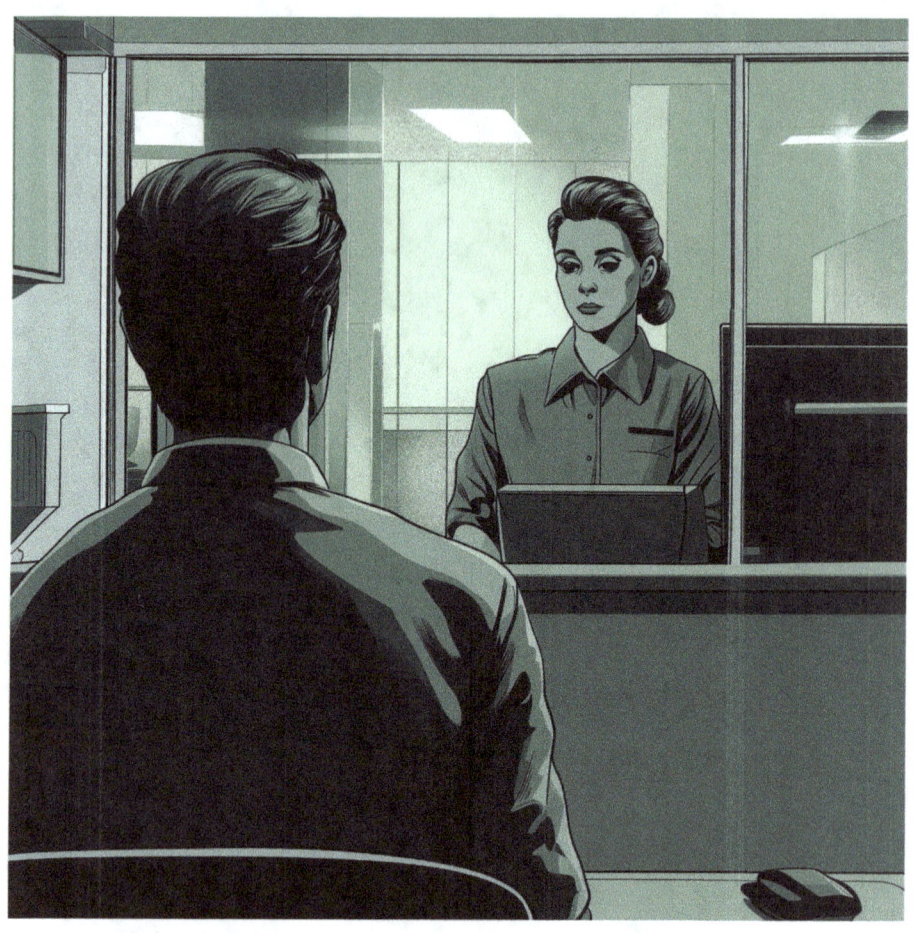

ONE OF A MAN'S HIGH POINTS IS: HIS BALANCE MAKES THE BANK TELLER CLENCH HER LEGS.

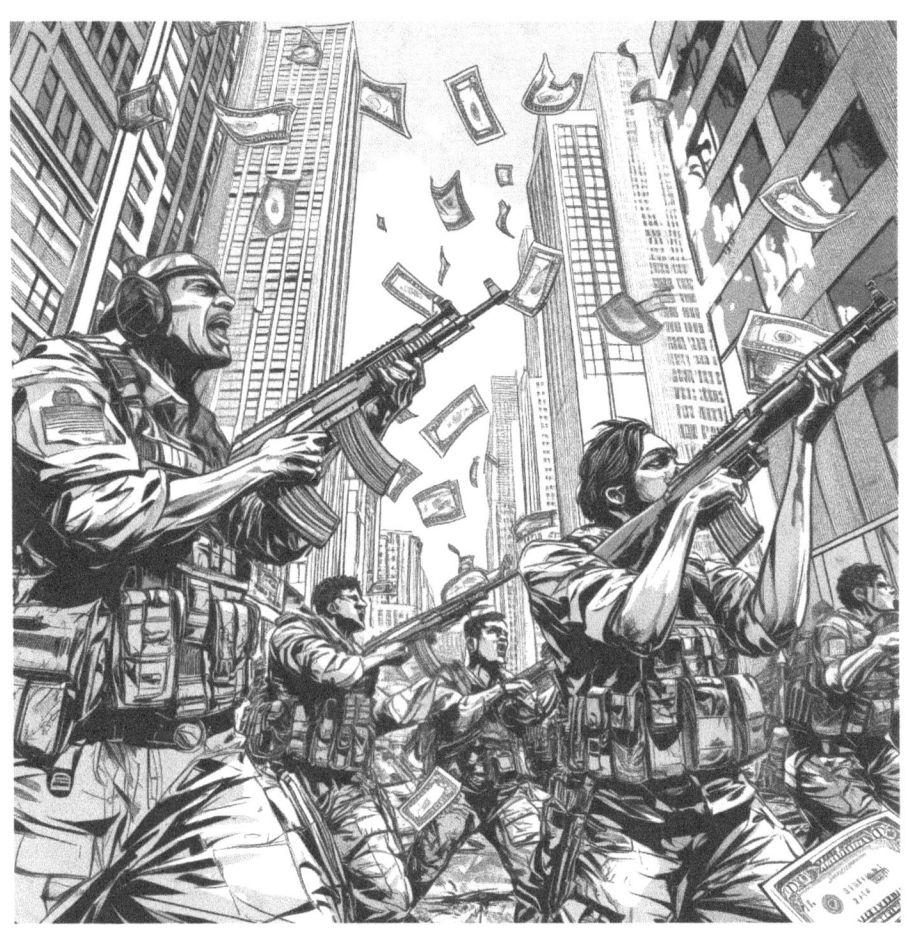

IT'S NOT A SUIT BUT A COMBAT UNIFORM. KEEP FIRING UNTIL MONEY'S BLOOD SPLASHES ON YOUR FACE AGAIN, AGAIN, AND AGAIN.

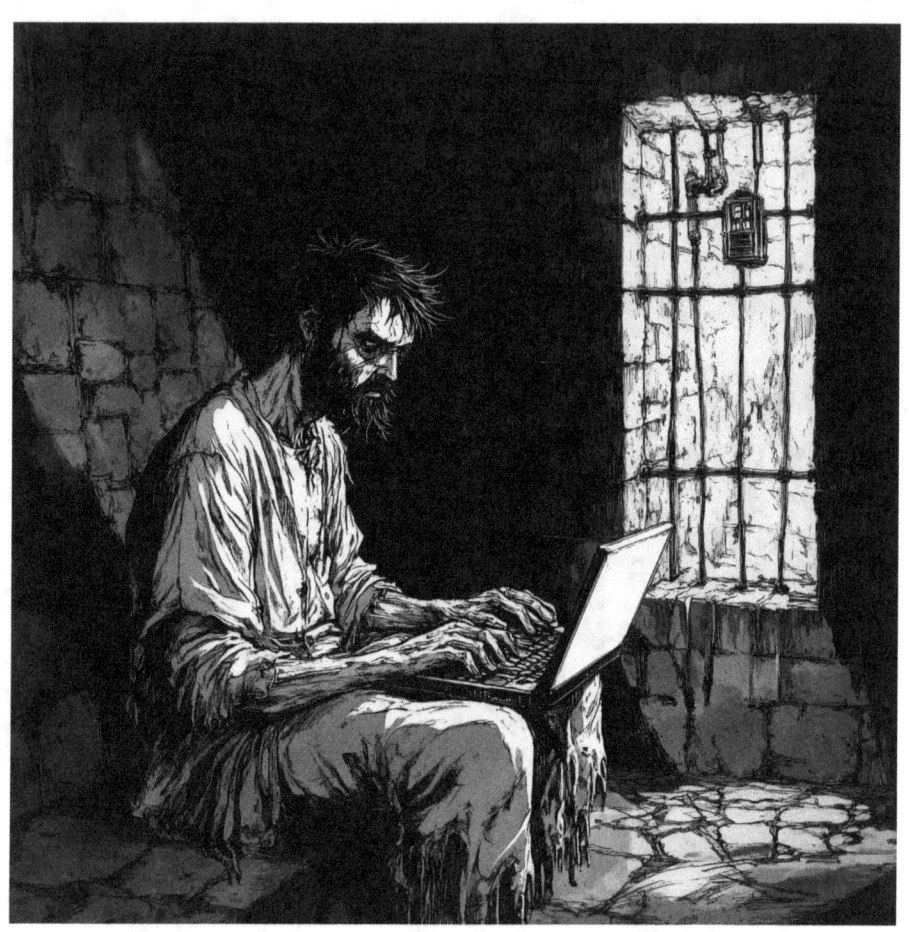

MAKE IT LIKE DANTÈS IN PRISON. SELL IT LIKE DANTÈS ON REVENGE.

STOP DANCING—RUN! THE WORLD LIVES ON WALL STREET—NOT AROUND THE CORNER AT BROADWAY.

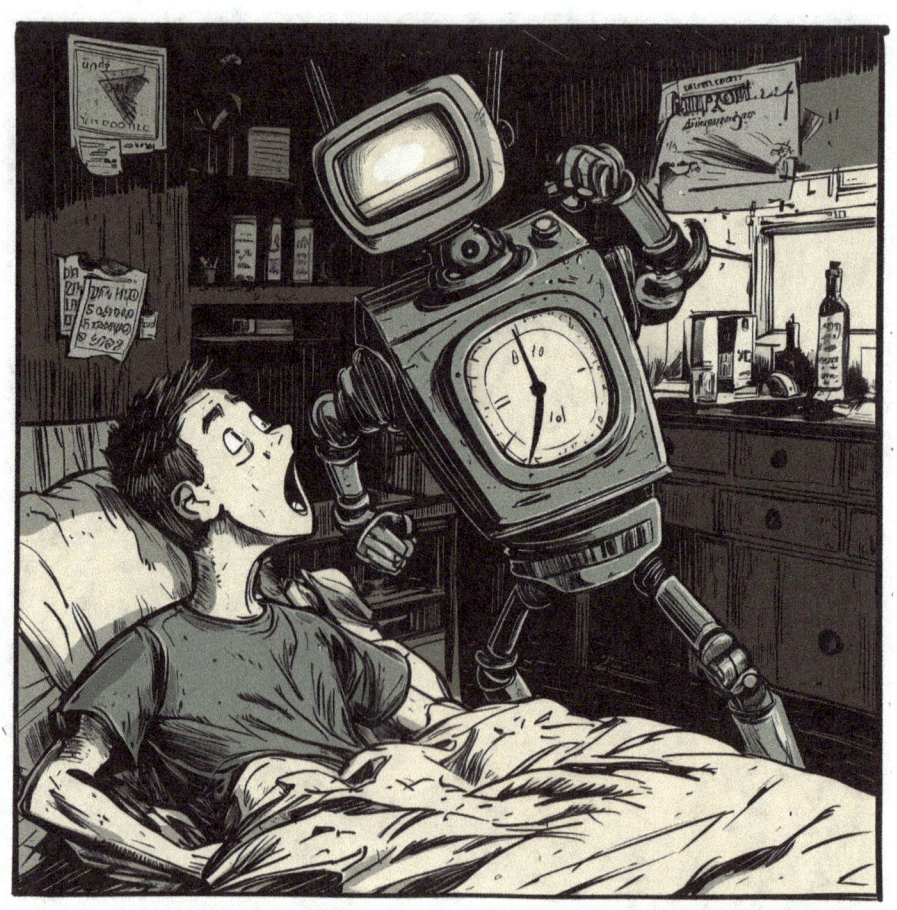

SET YOUR ALARM TO SAY: PROM'S OVER, BIG SHOT— GET UP AND EARN YOUR BREAKFAST!

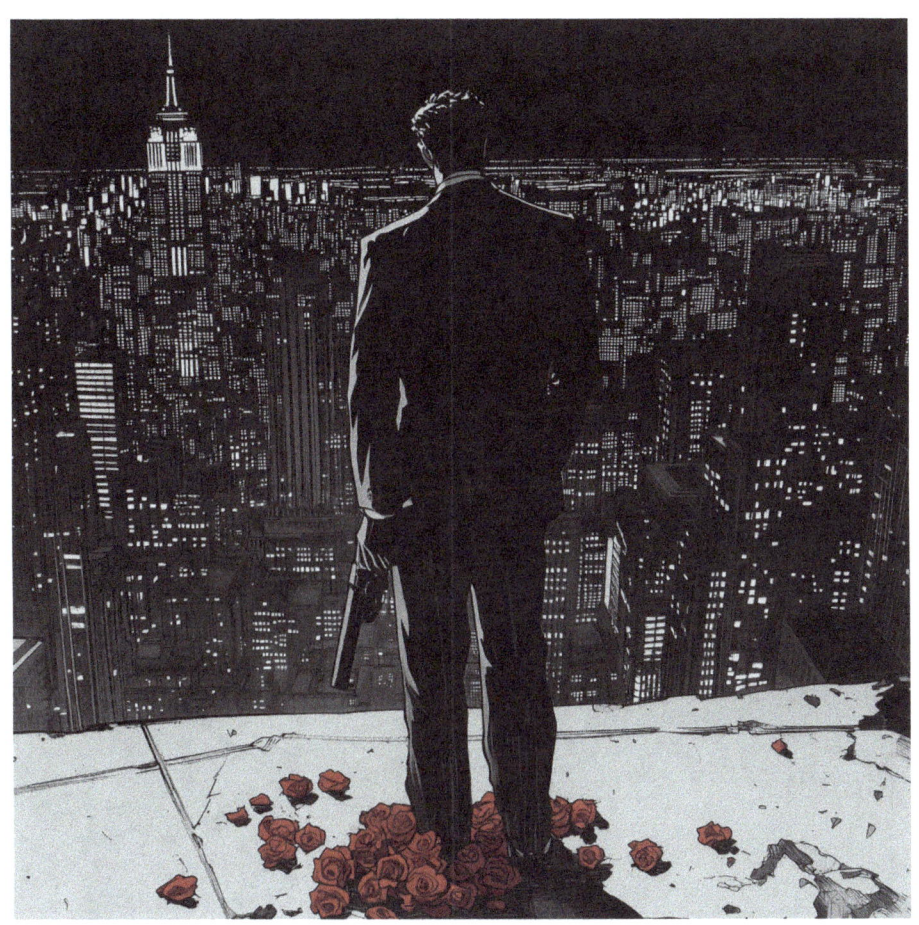

IF A BUSINESS BOOK READS BEAUTIFULLY, IT WAS WRITTEN BY A WRITER—NOT A BUSINESSMAN. DON'T READ IT.

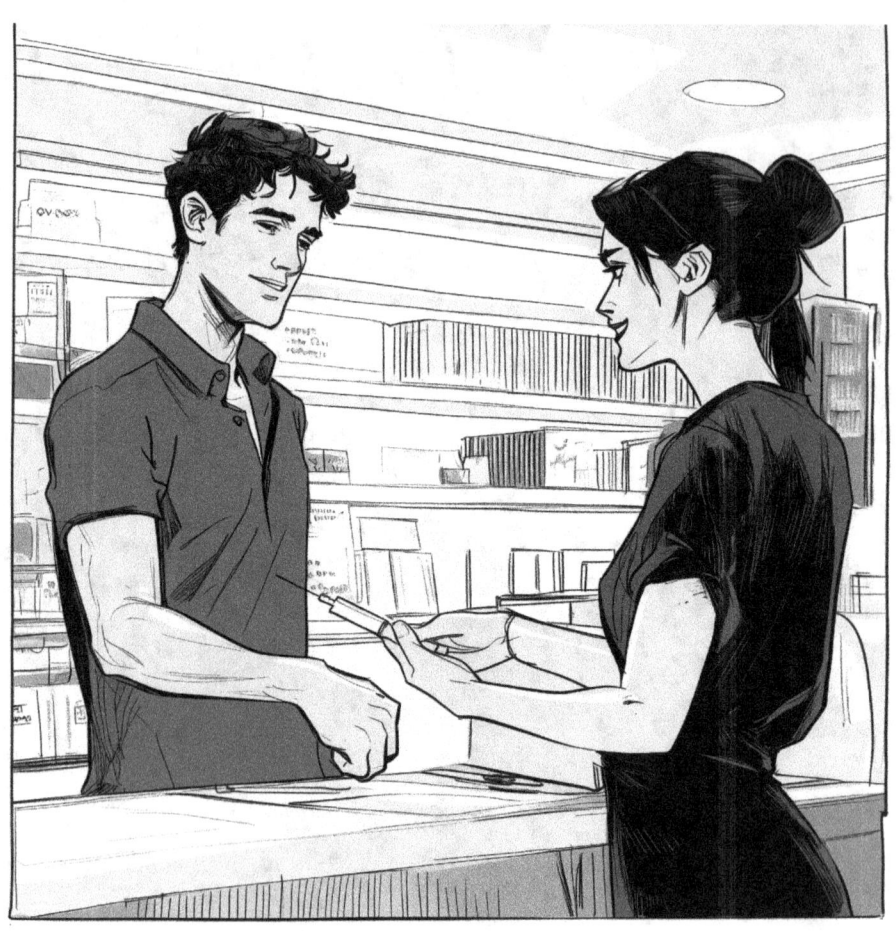

CALL THE DOLLAR "CC." IMAGINE EVERY SHHK OF YOUR CARD IS A VEIN CUT.

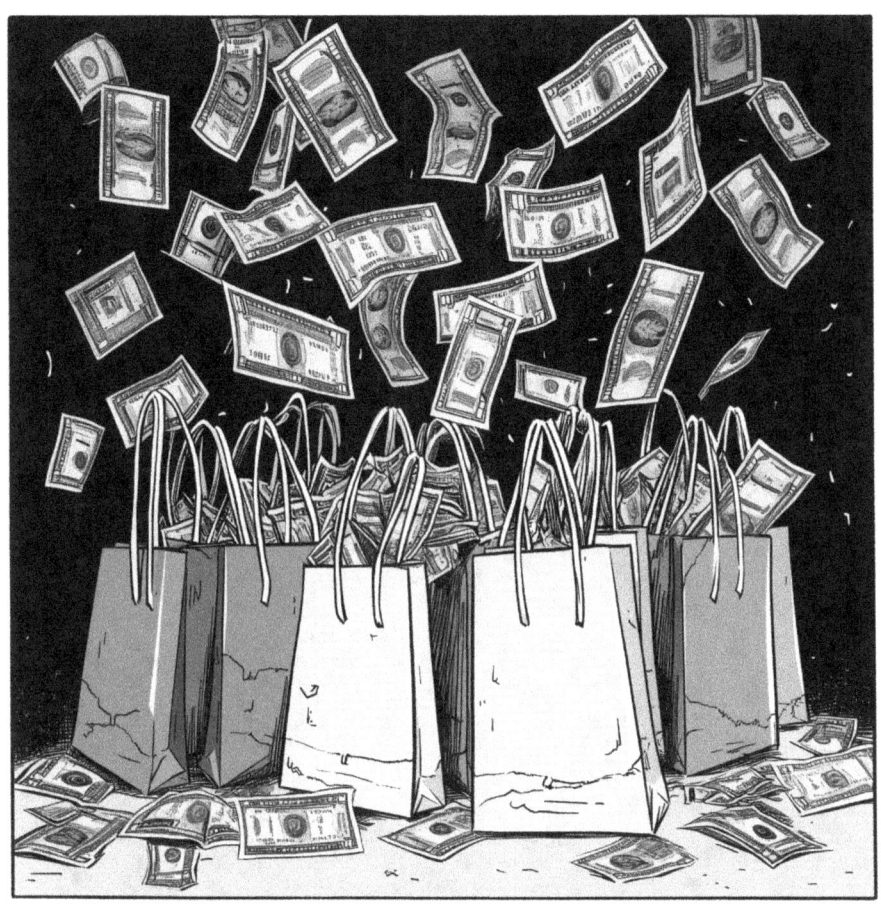

THE ONE WHO STOLE YOUR LUXURY BAG ISN'T THE THIEF—THE ONE WHO SOLD IT TO YOU IS.

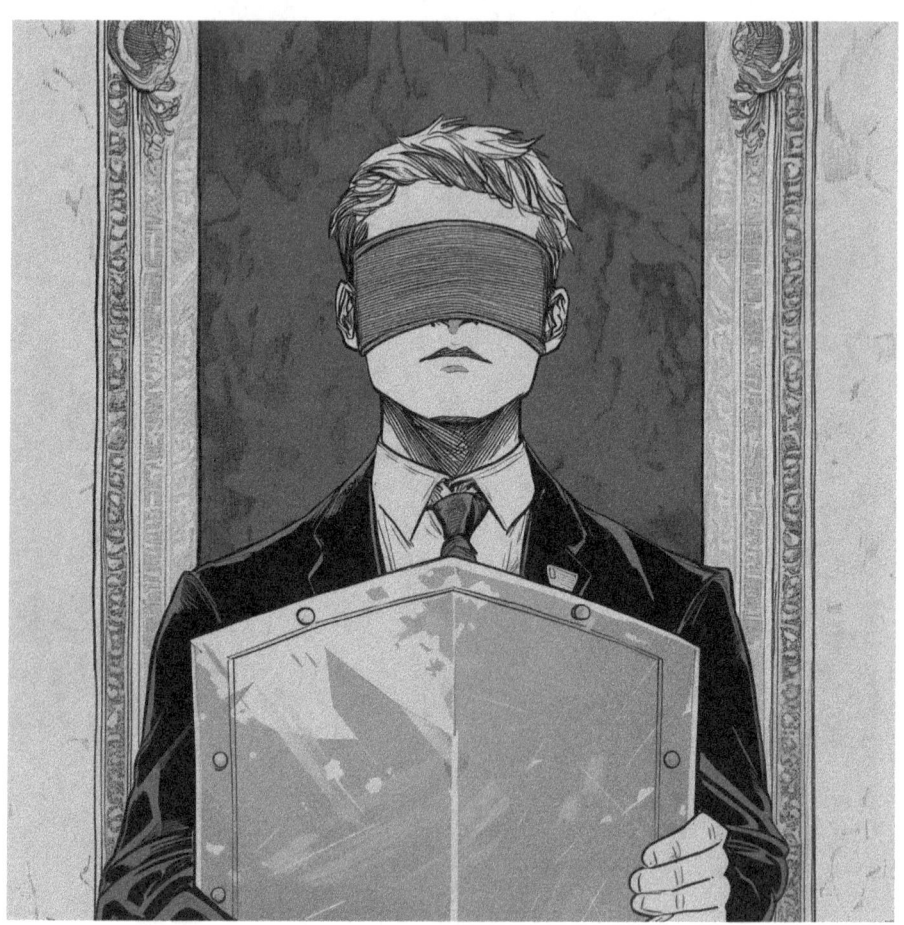

NEVER PAY FOR A SALESPERSON'S SMILE.

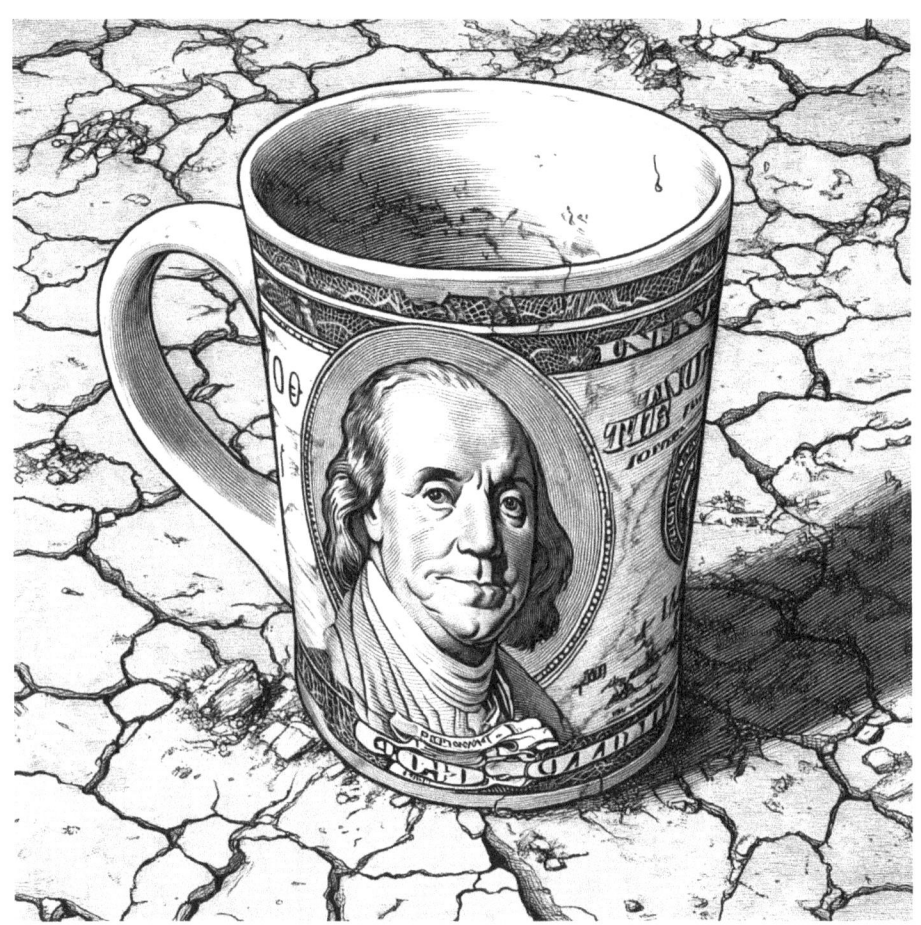

DON'T BUY AN EXPENSIVE CUP JUST TO DRINK BETTER WATER.

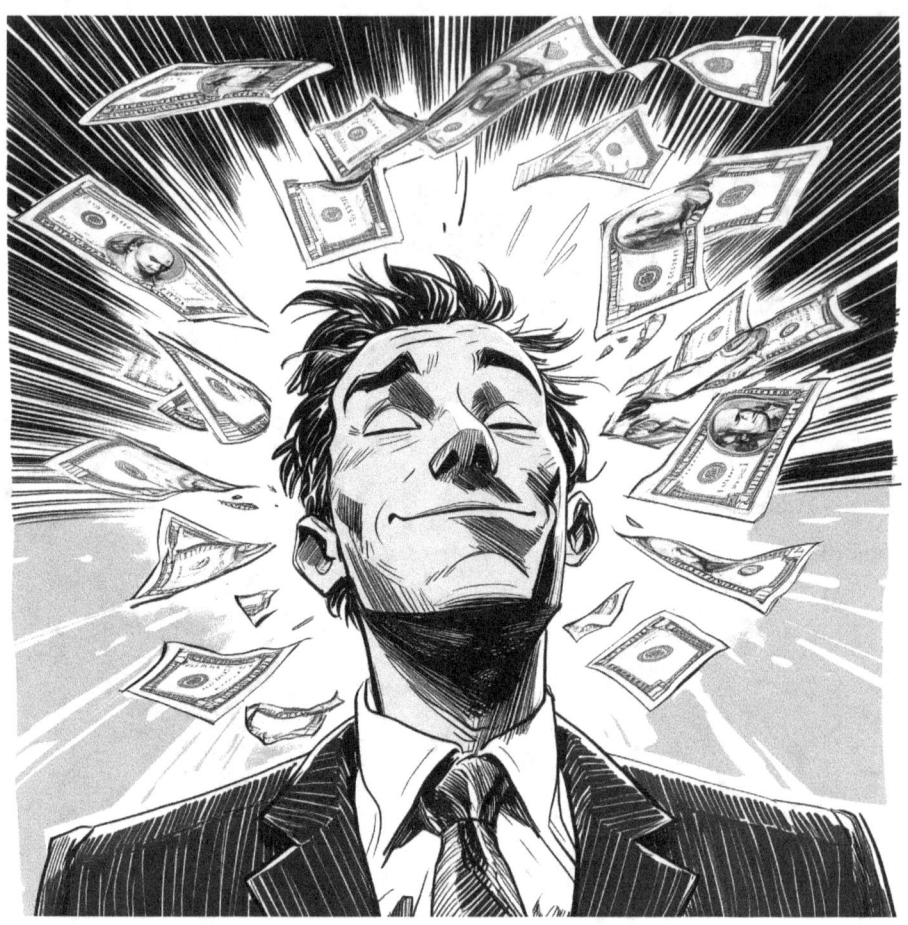

IF YOU HEAR PRAISE AS AN ADULT, YOU'VE DEFINITELY OVERPAID FOR SOMETHING.

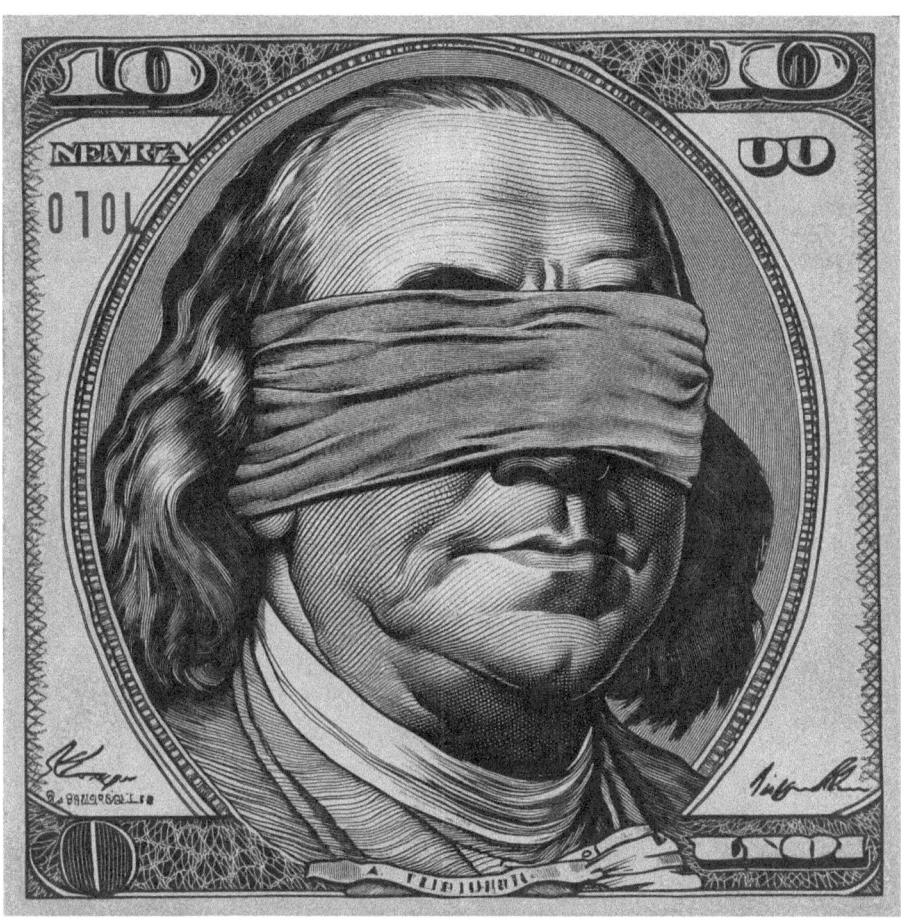

KEEP EVERY NON-PROFITABLE STRANGER A STRANGER.

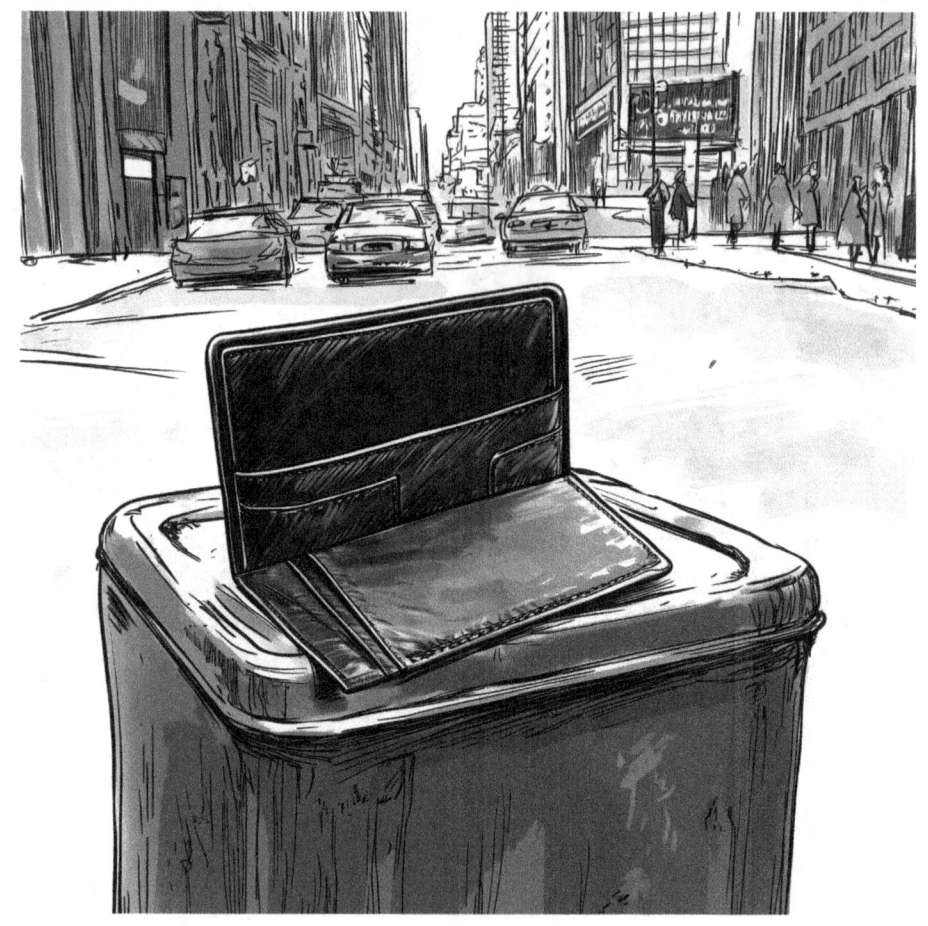

A WALLET ISN'T AN ASSET. MONEY IS.

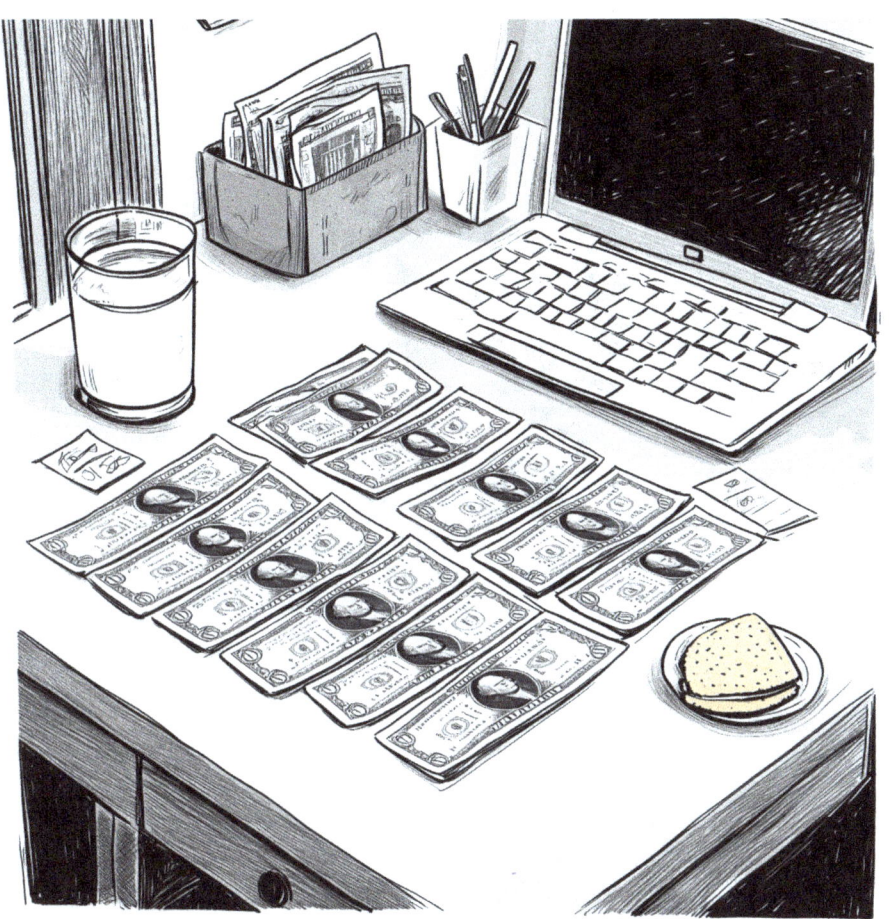

SWITCH ALL AUTO-RENEWALS TO MANUAL.

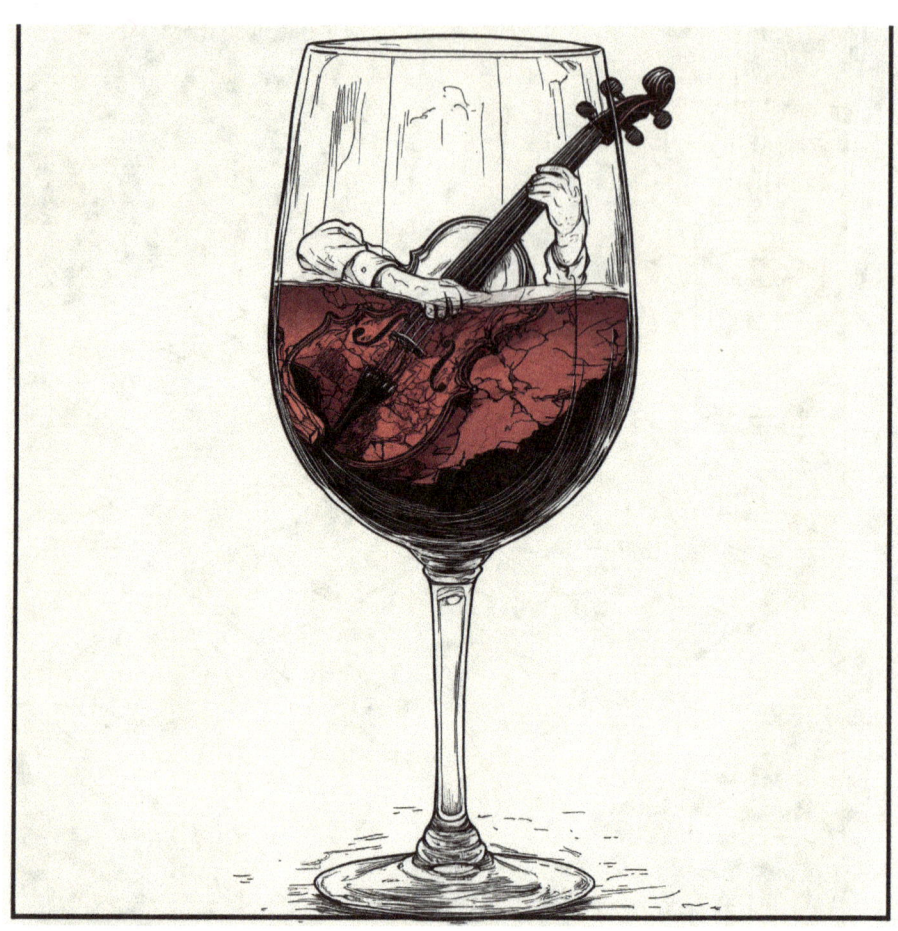

UNTIL IT MAKES MONEY, EVERY HOBBY IS A VICE.

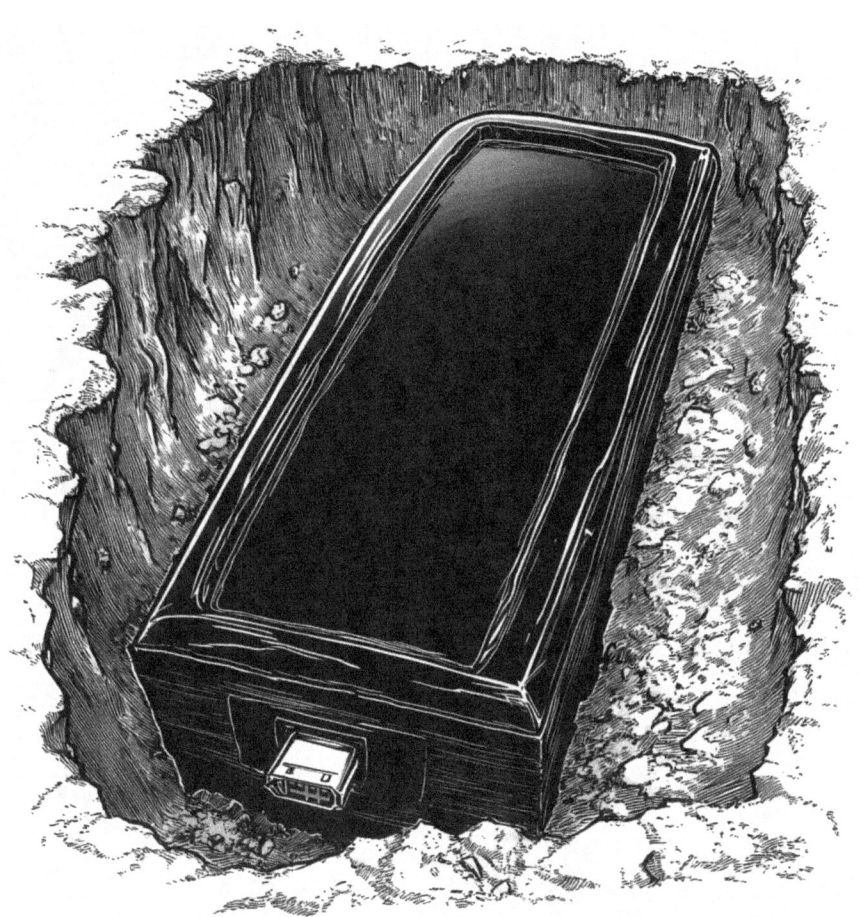

CUT EVERY PLAN NOT FOR MONEY INTO A COFFIN-SHAPED FLASH DRIVE.

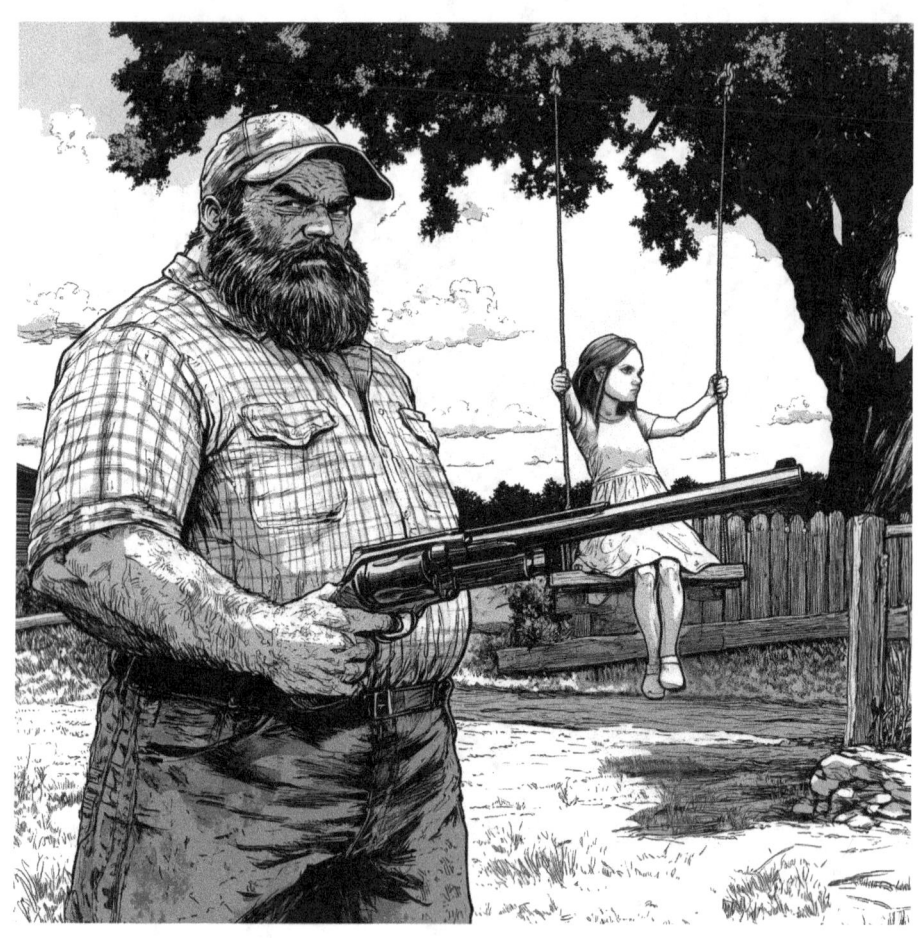

GUARD YOUR CASH LIKE IT'S YOUR UNMARRIED DAUGHTER.

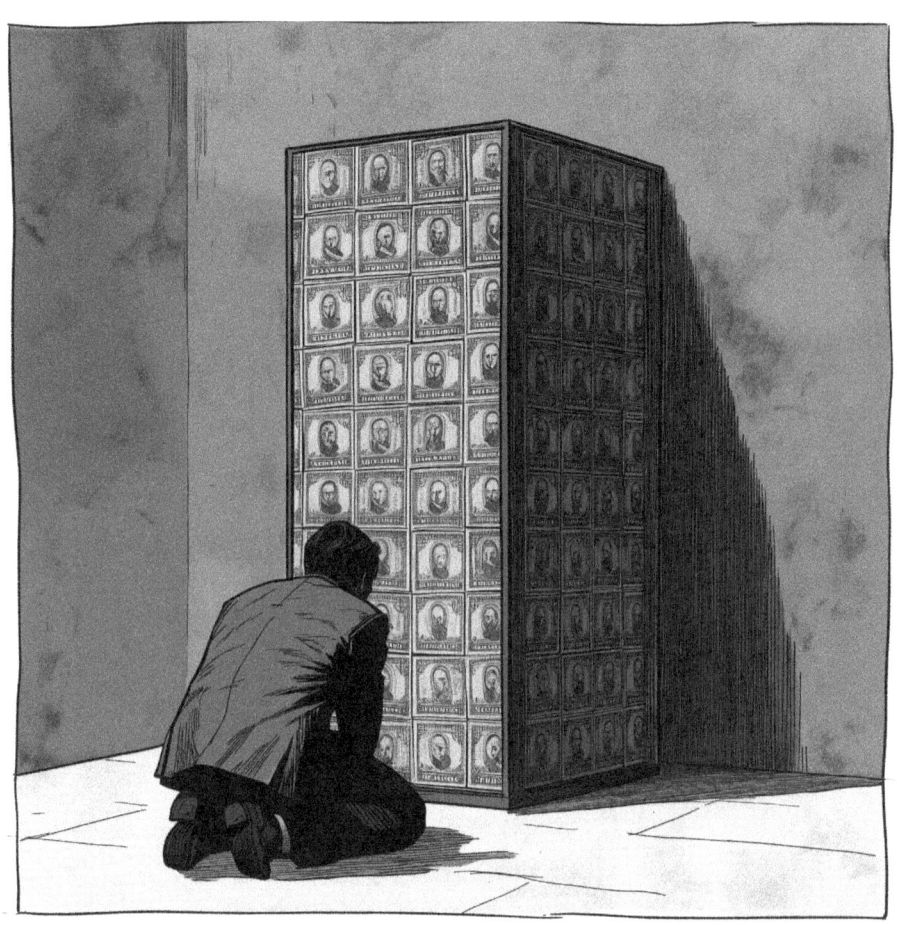

IF A PAYOUT DOESN'T MAKE YOU FEEL GUILTY – YOU ASKED TOO LITTLE.

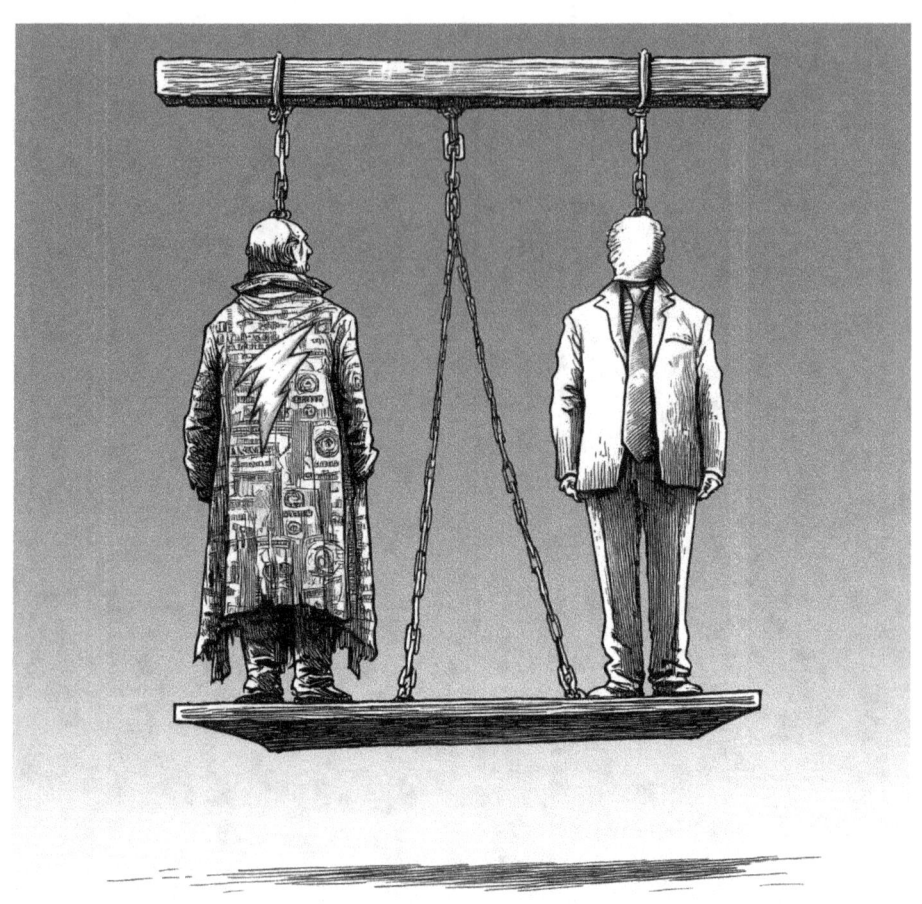

HANG YOUR GET-RICH-QUICK PLAN BEFORE IT HANGS YOU.

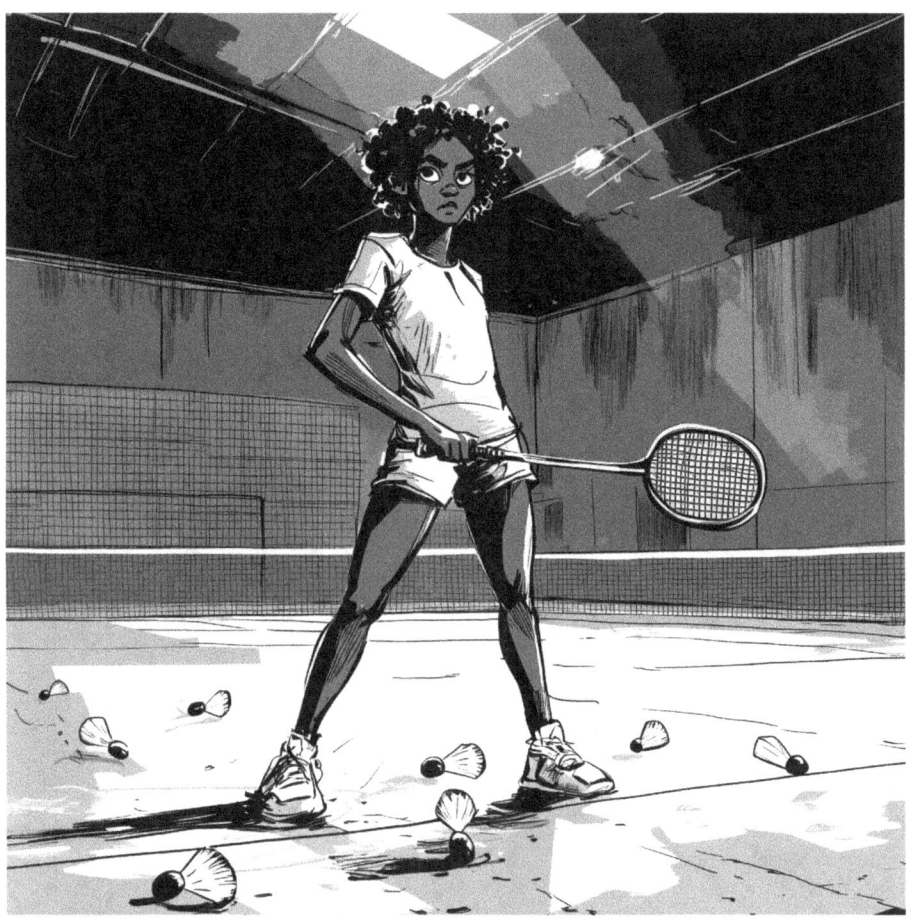

START WITH TRIAL AND ERROR—NOT HESITATION.

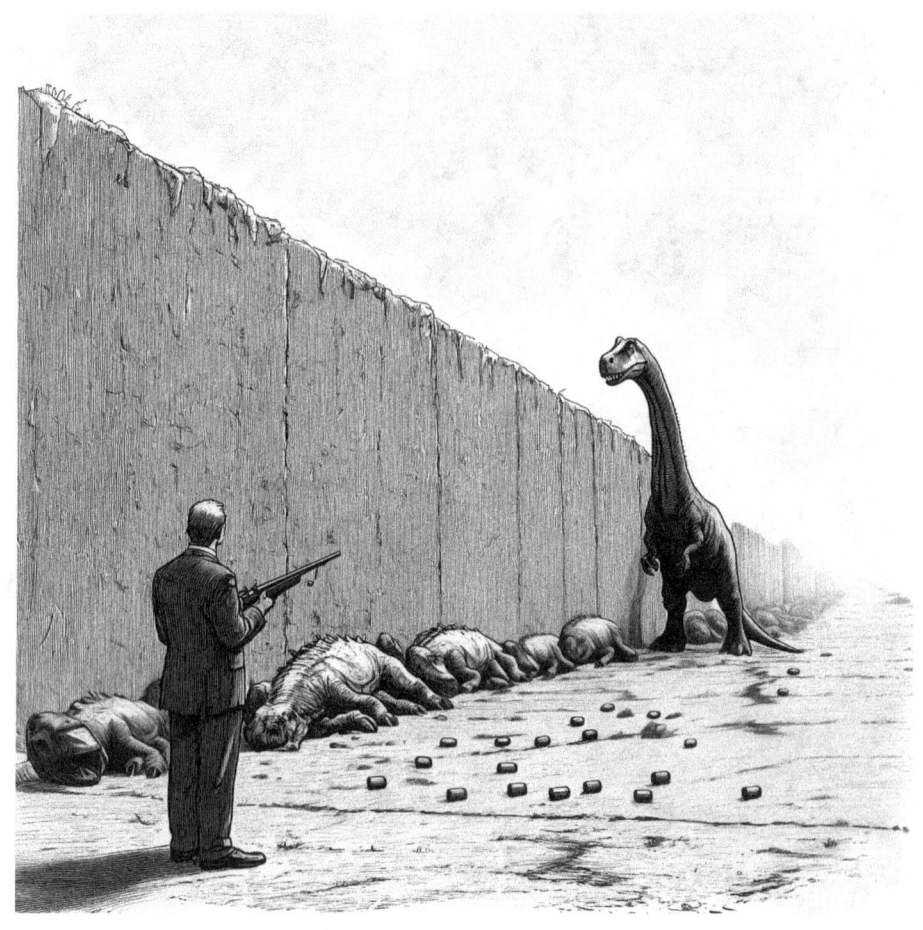

EXECUTE ALL IDEAS BUT SPARE ONE.

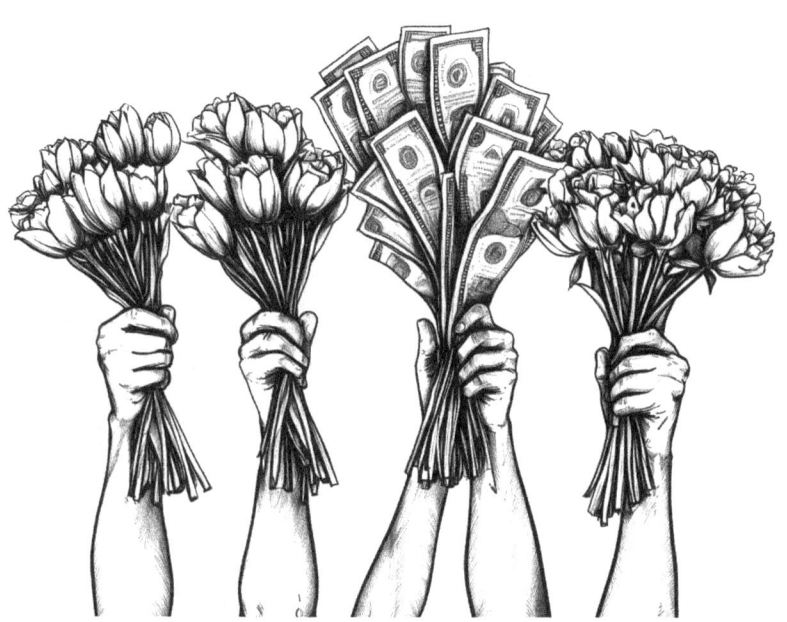

ONLY ONE KIND OF PRAISE IS REAL—A PAYOUT.

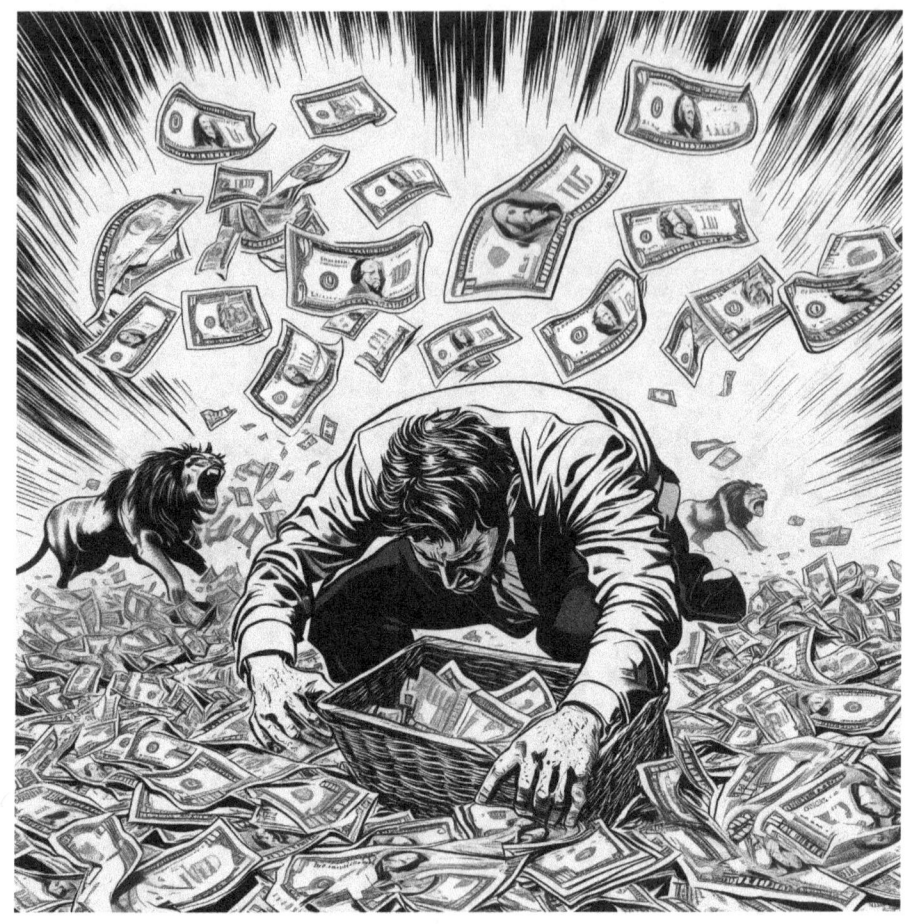

WORK THROUGH THE NOISE. CASH THROUGH THE CHAOS.

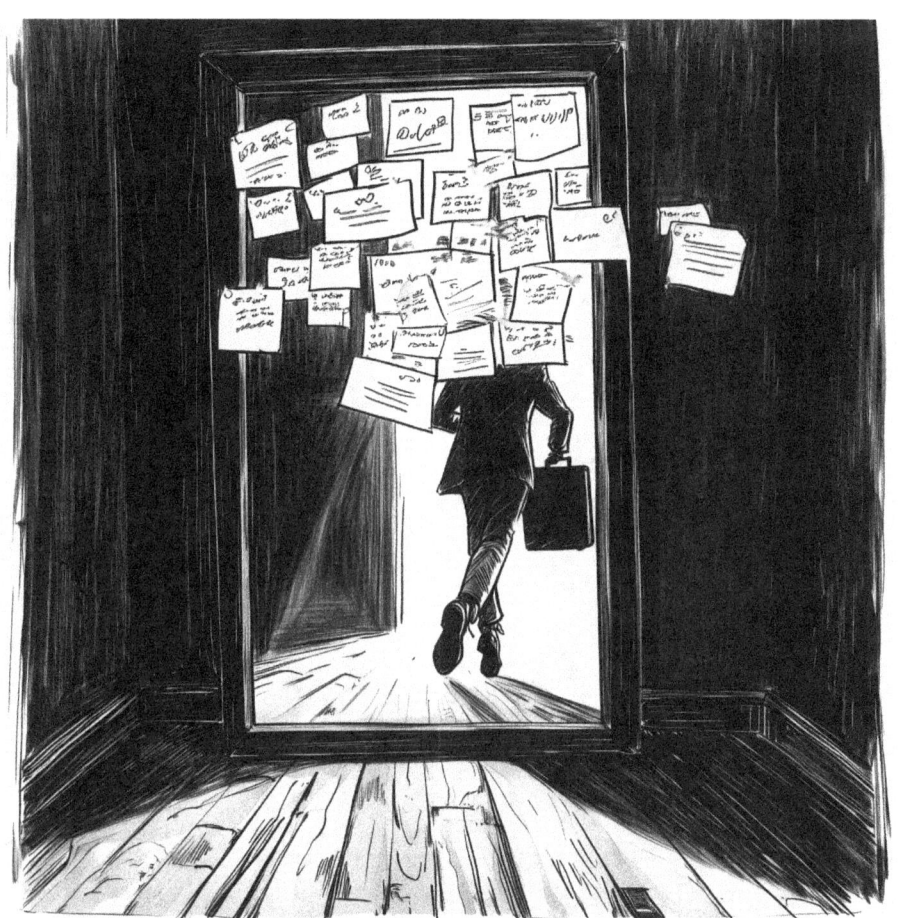

WRITE YOUR TO-DO LIST ON YOUR FULL-LENGTH MIRROR.

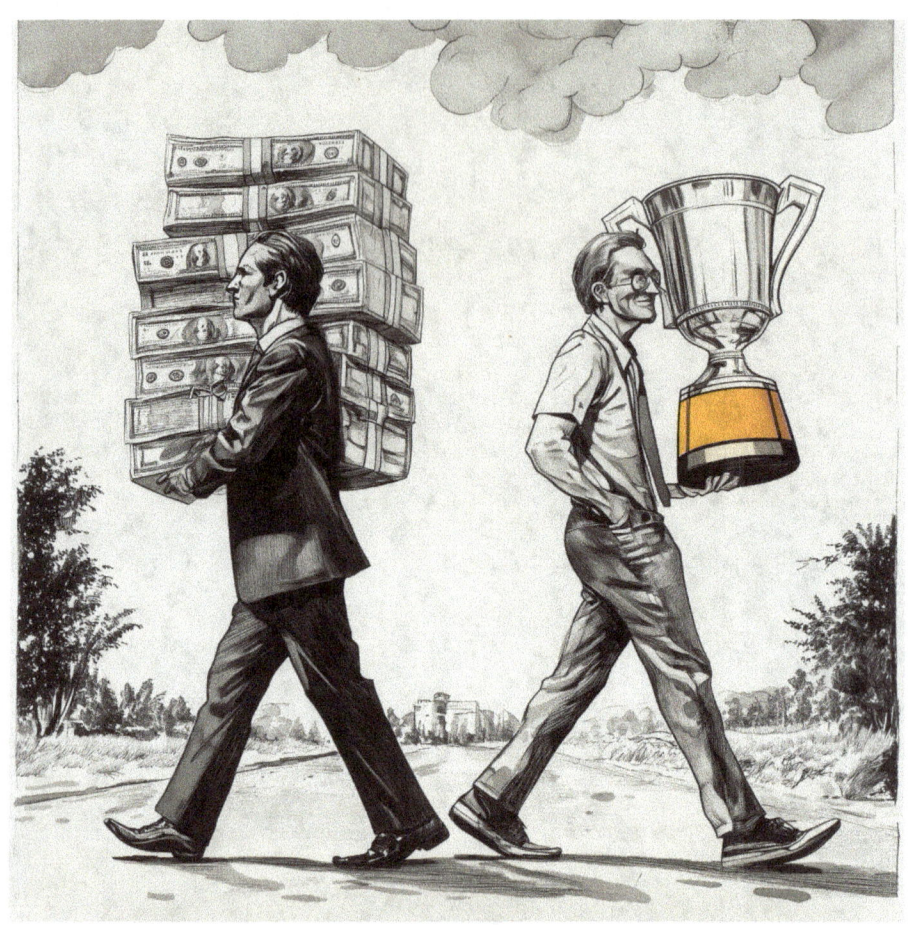

LET THEM WIN. YOU GET PAID.

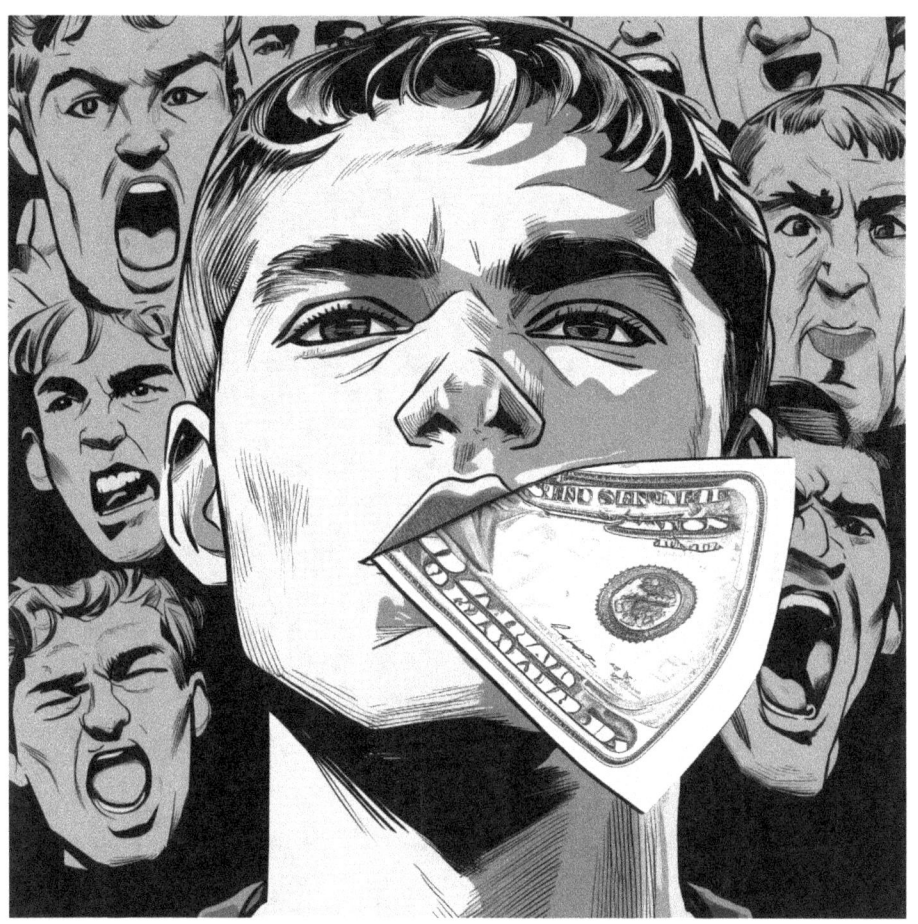

THEY BRAG. YOU SHUT UP.

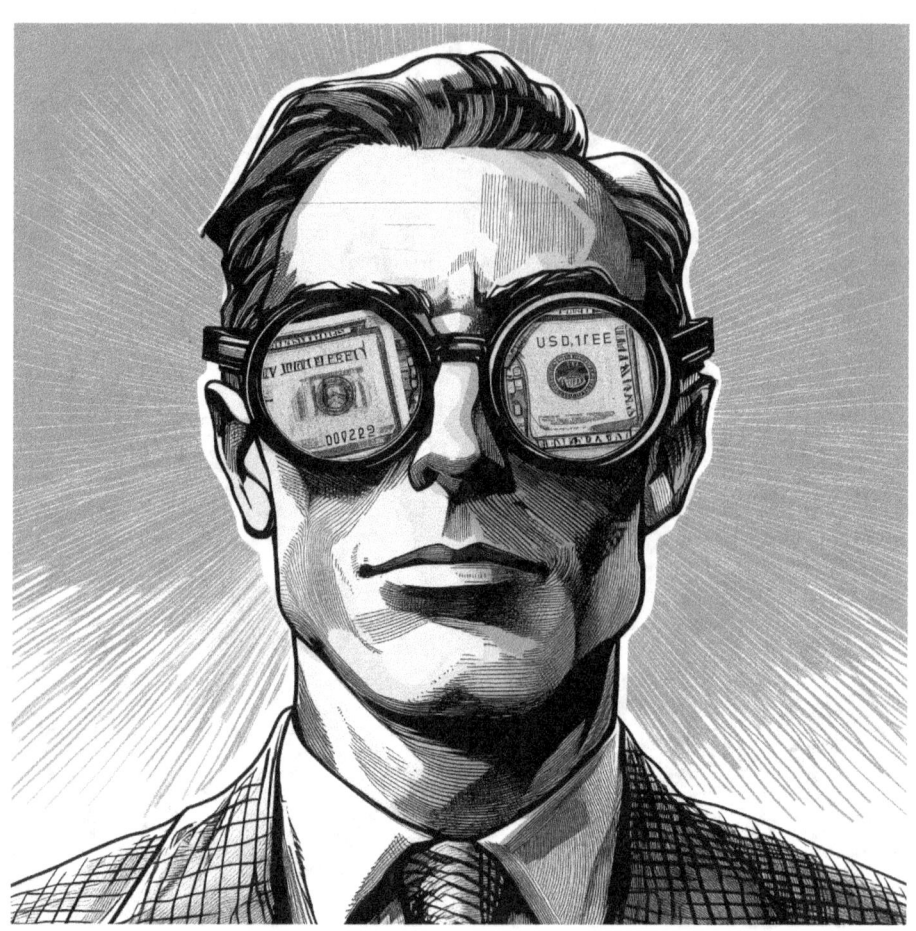

IF IT DOESN'T PAY YOU, IT DOESN'T EXIST.

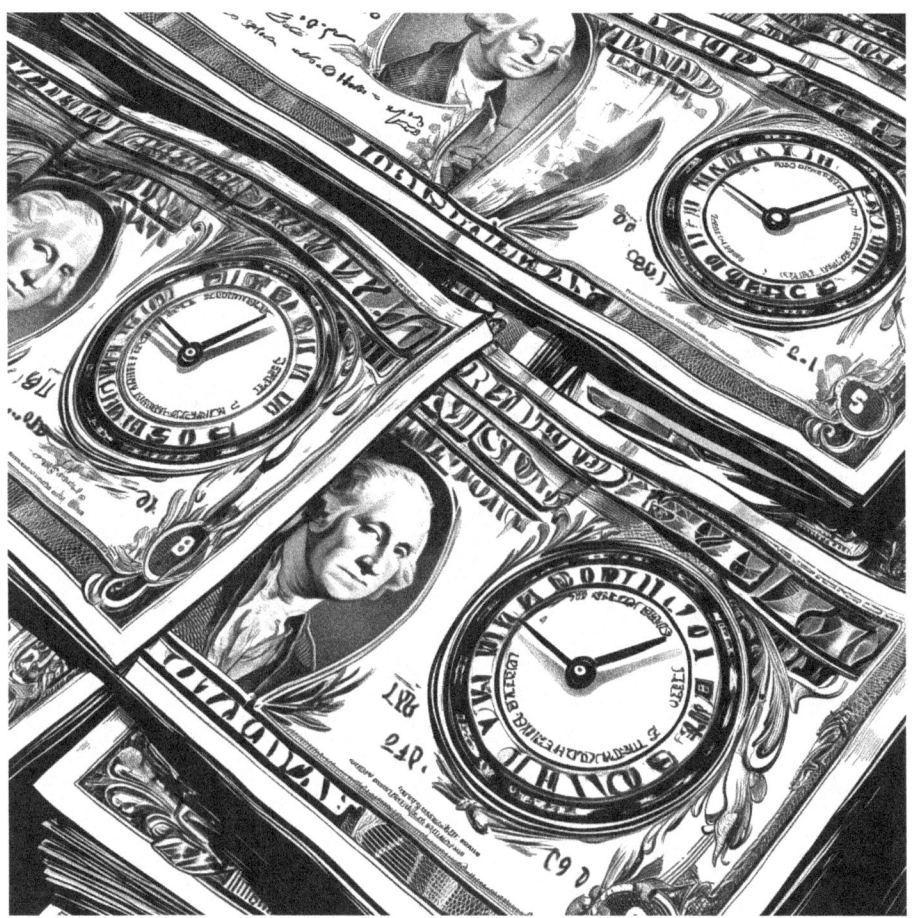

TREAT YOUR TIME LIKE IT'S CASH.

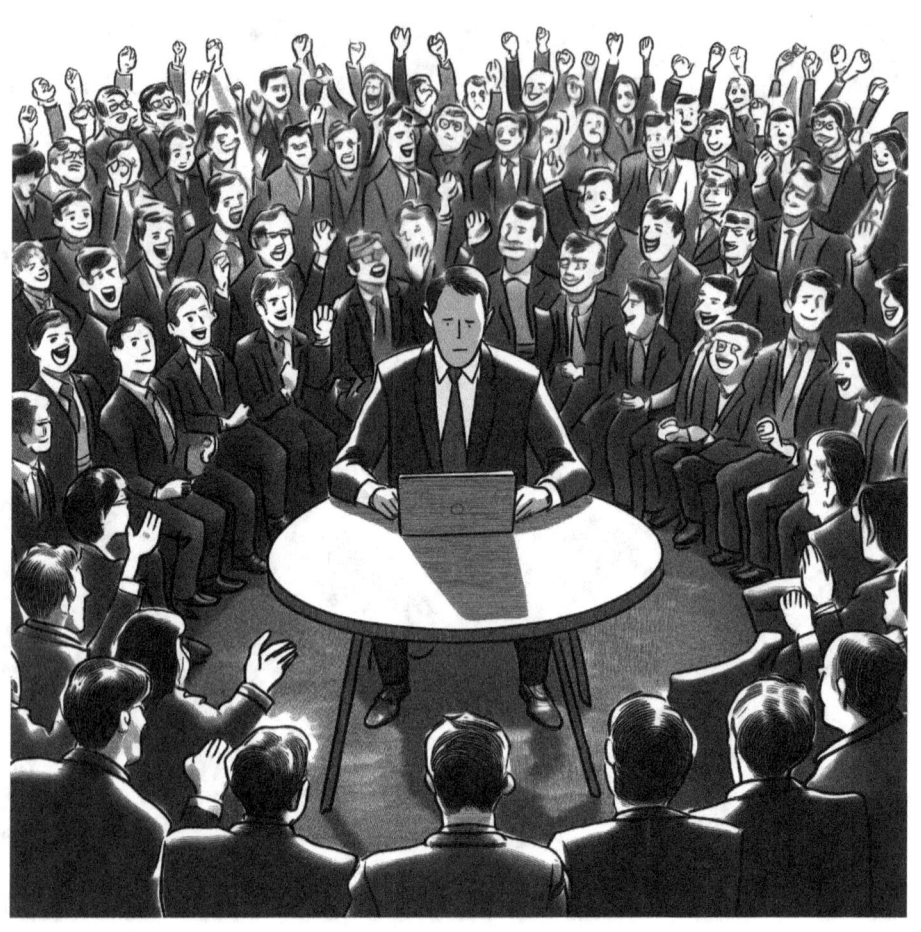

ALWAYS IGNORE THE AUDIENCE.

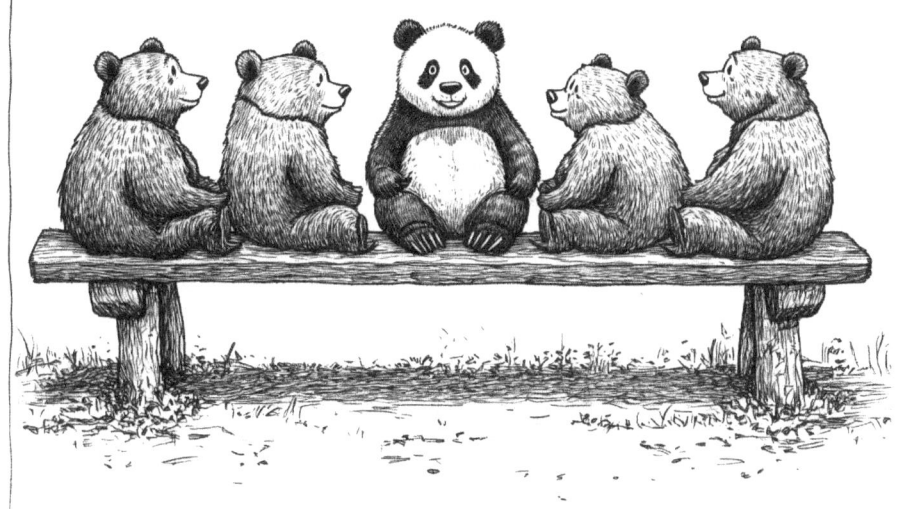

DON'T BECOME CHEAPER—BECOME RARER.

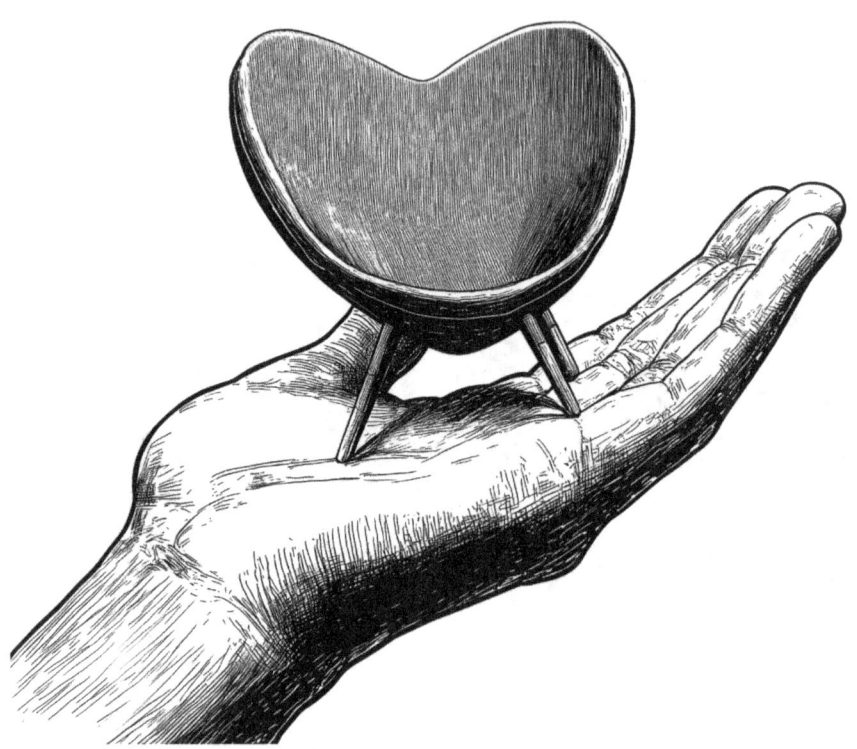

DON'T OFFER YOUR HEART. OFFER A PRODUCT.

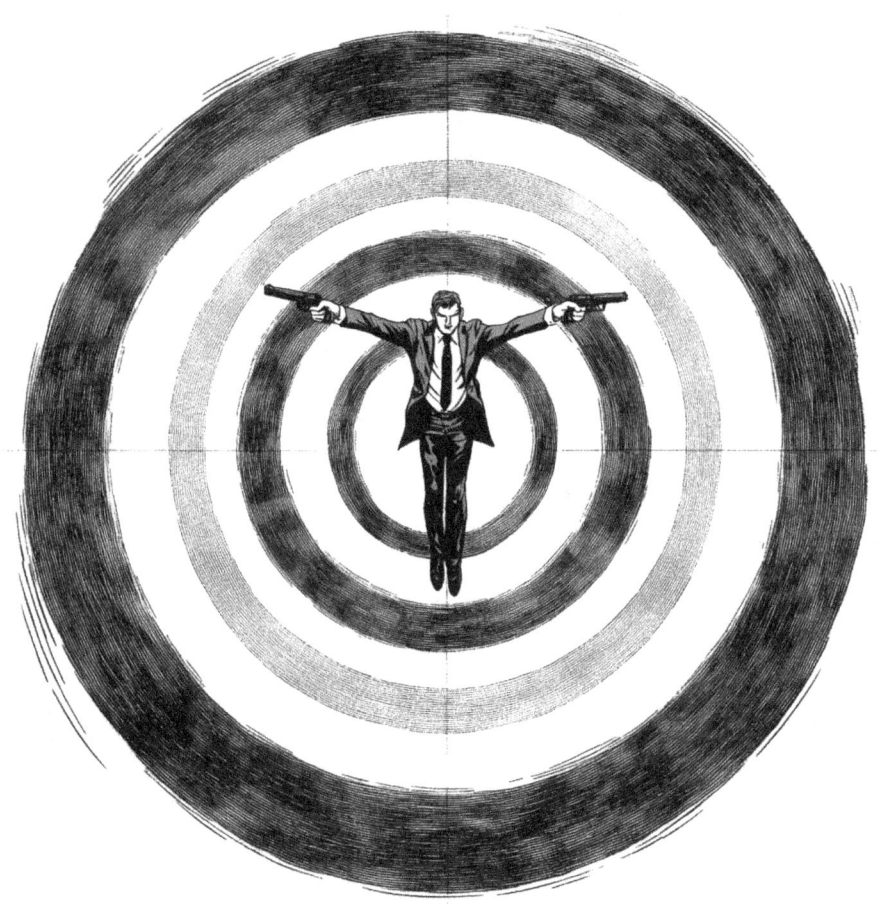

ATTENTION IS YOUR CORE ASSET. ONCE IT'S SCATTERED, THE REST SOON FOLLOWS.

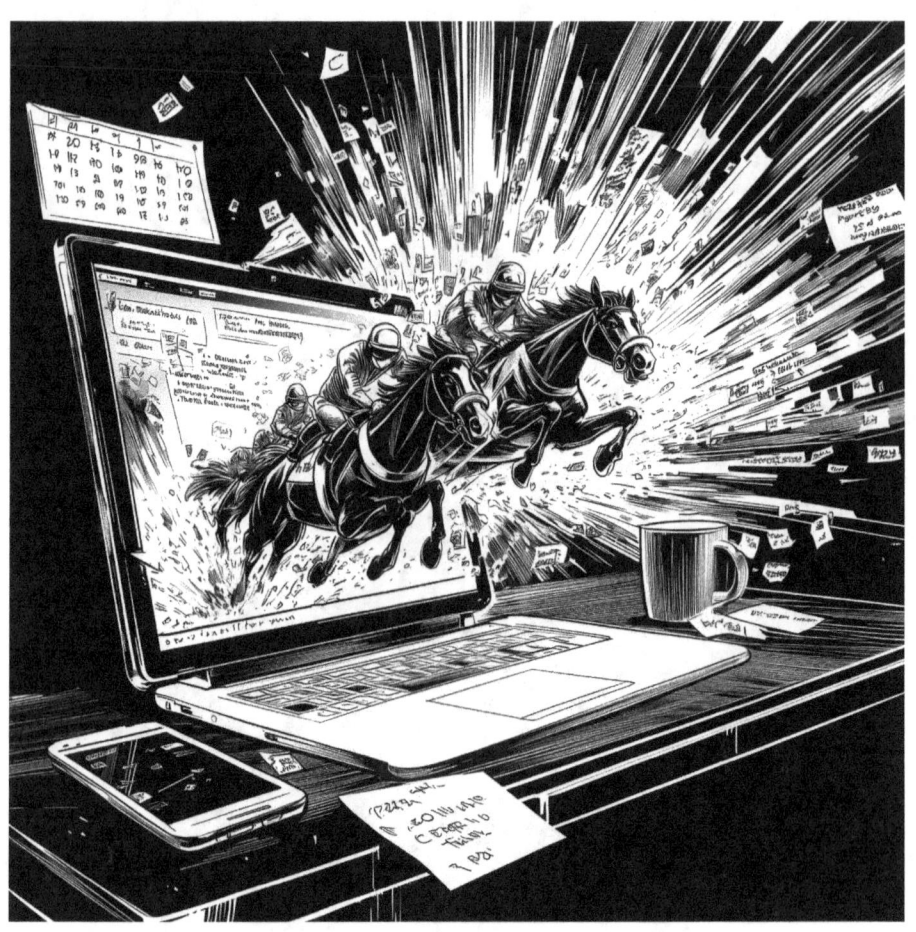

SET YOUR WALLPAPER TO A PROGRESS CHART.

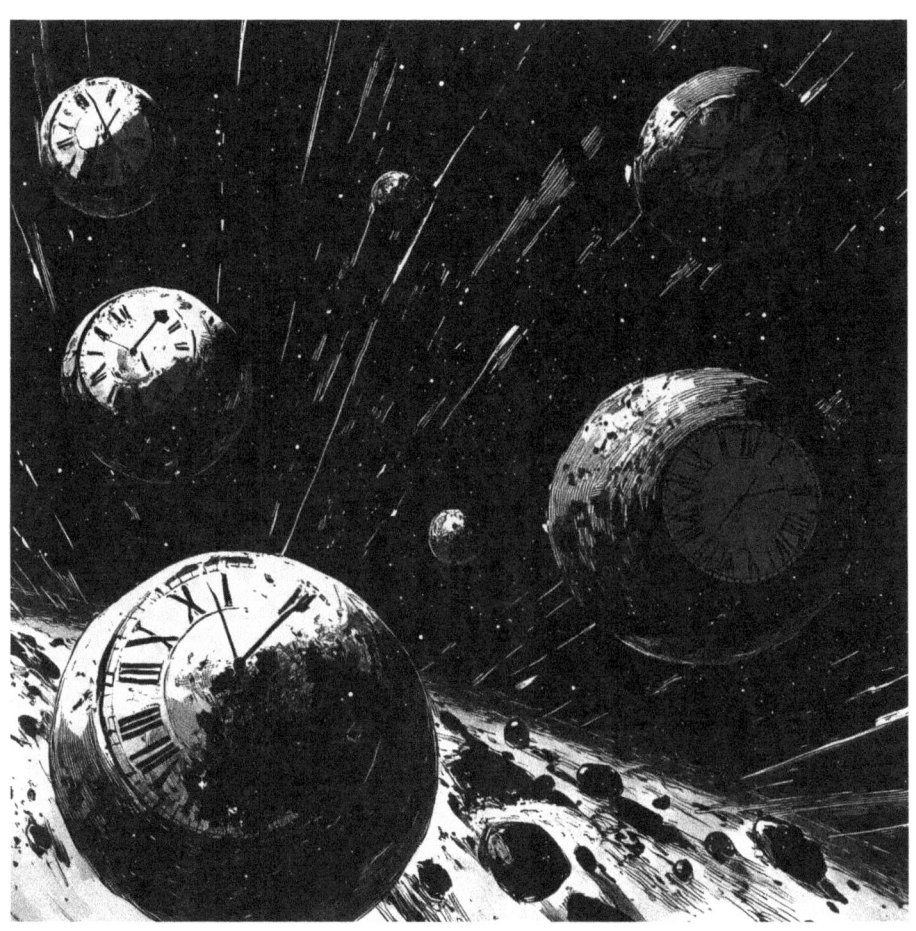

NEVER FORGET—TIME IS THE SNEAKIEST VARIABLE IN EVERY PLAN.

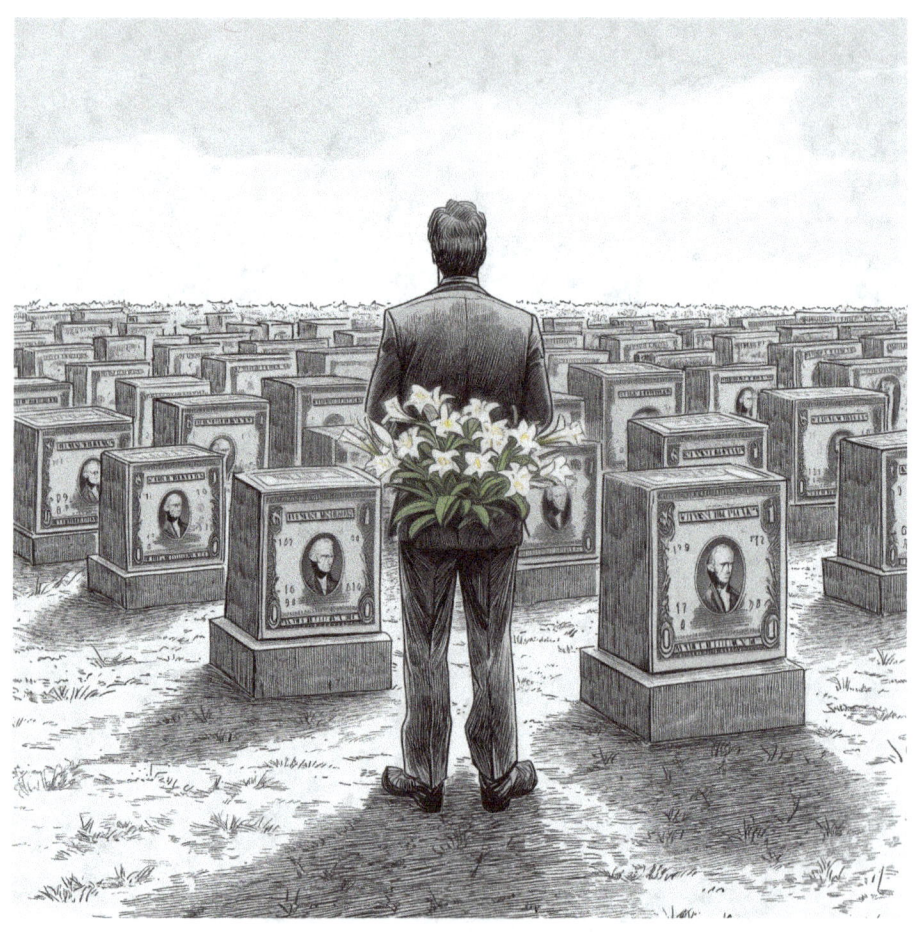

NEATLY RECORD EVERY DOLLAR YOU SPEND.

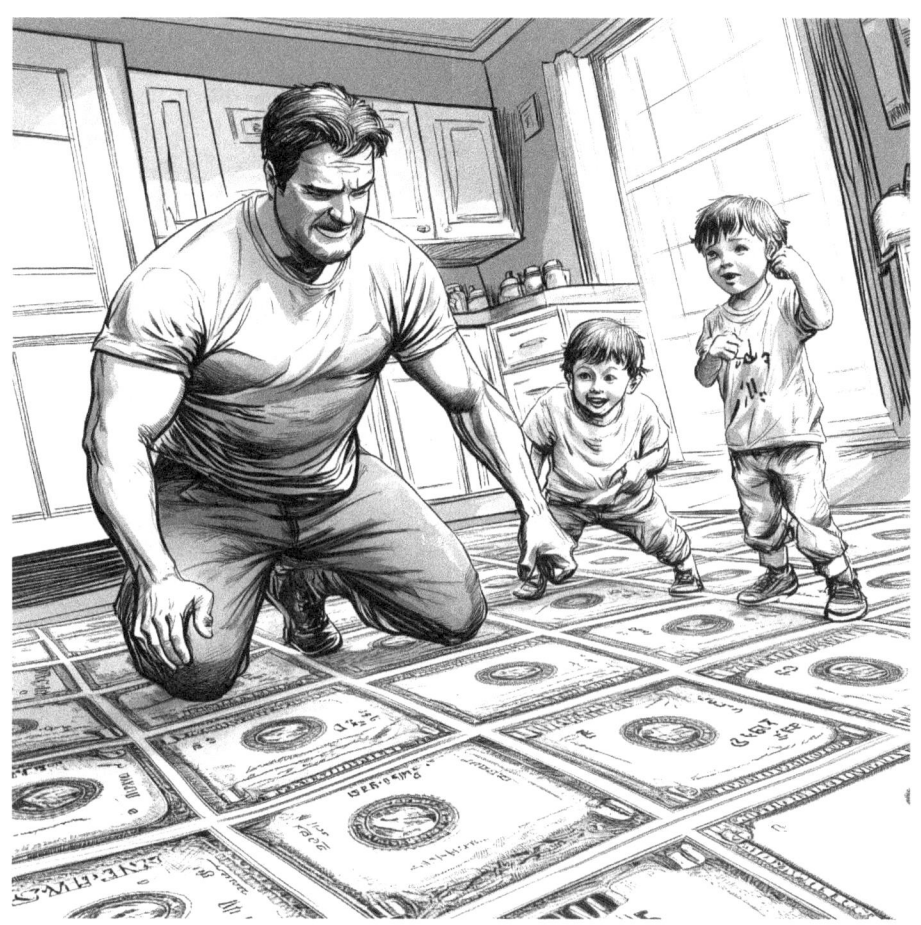

STOP BUYING FITNESS. DO FREE PUSH-UPS ON YOUR OWN FLOOR.

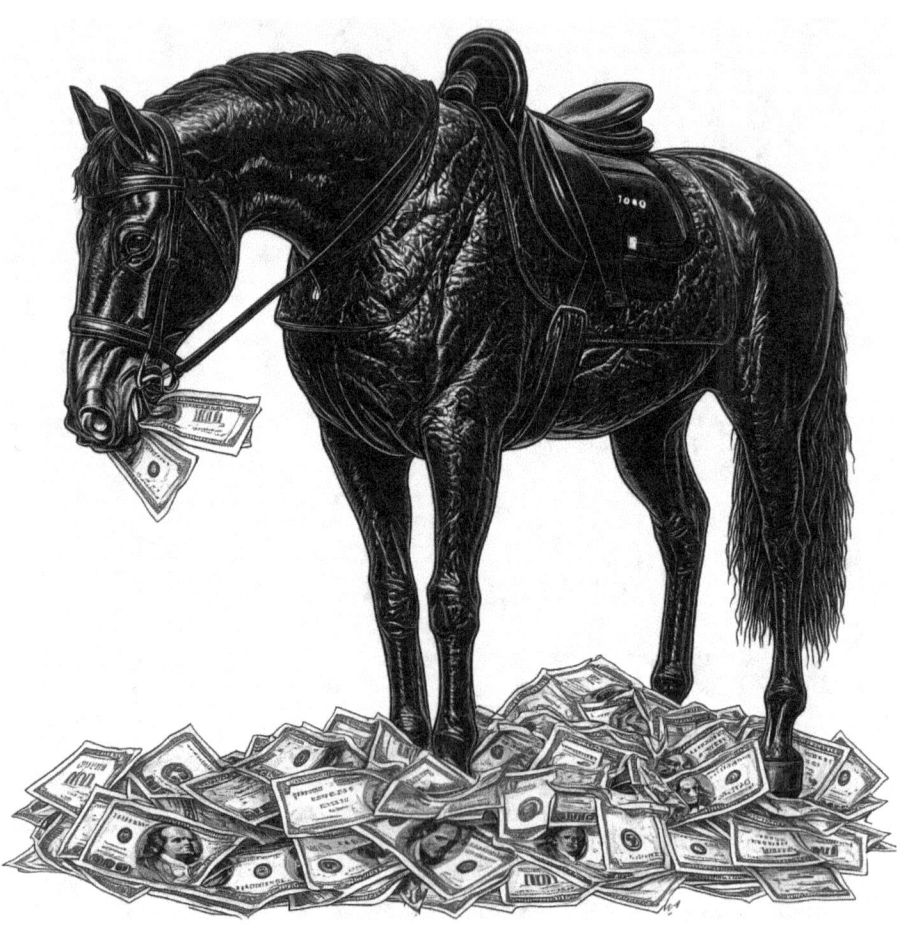

LUXURY MAY NOT MAKE YOU LOOK RICH—BUT IT DOES MAKE YOU POOR.

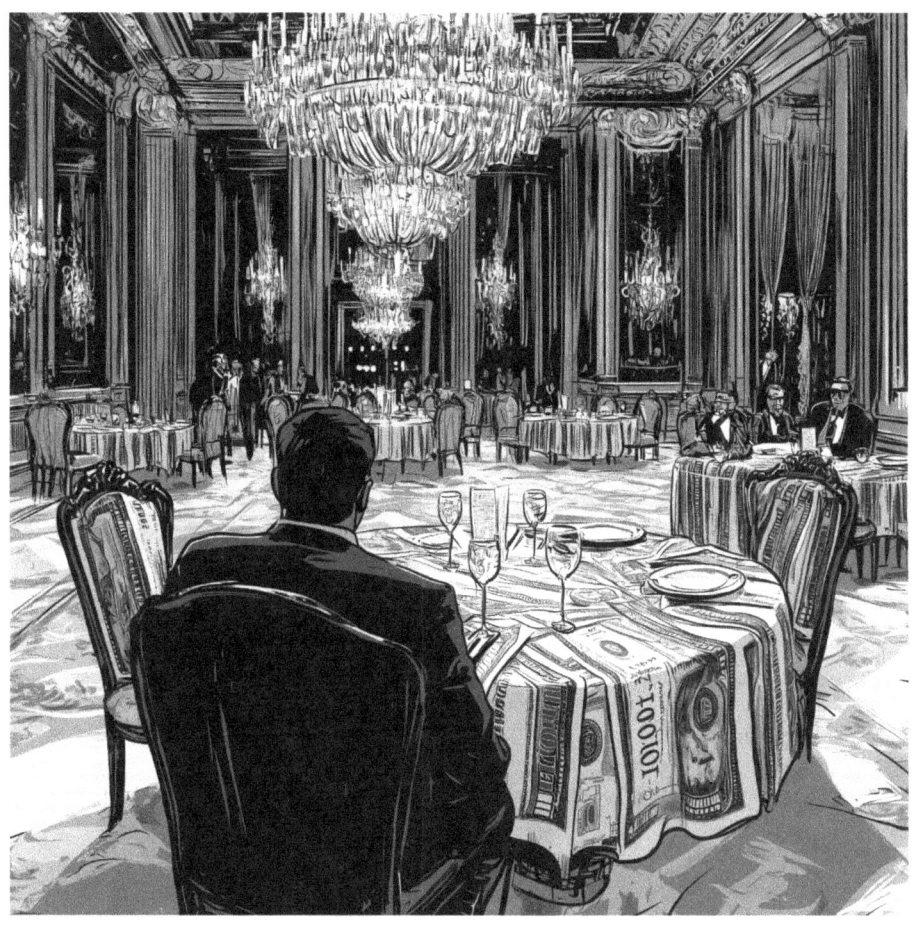

JUST A REMINDER: THE CHANDELIER AT THE RESTAURANT ADDS ZERO PROTEIN TO YOUR FOOD.

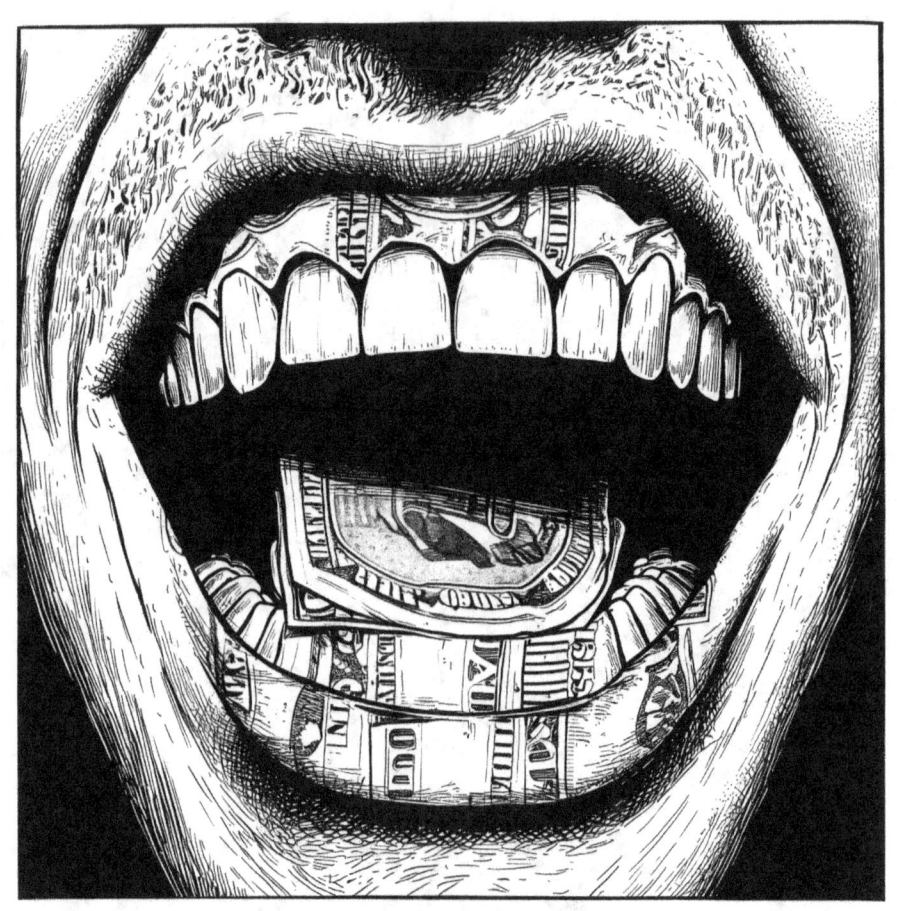

THE PRODUCT IS WORTH NOTHING. WHAT THEY PAY FOR IS YOUR NERVE TO SELL IT.

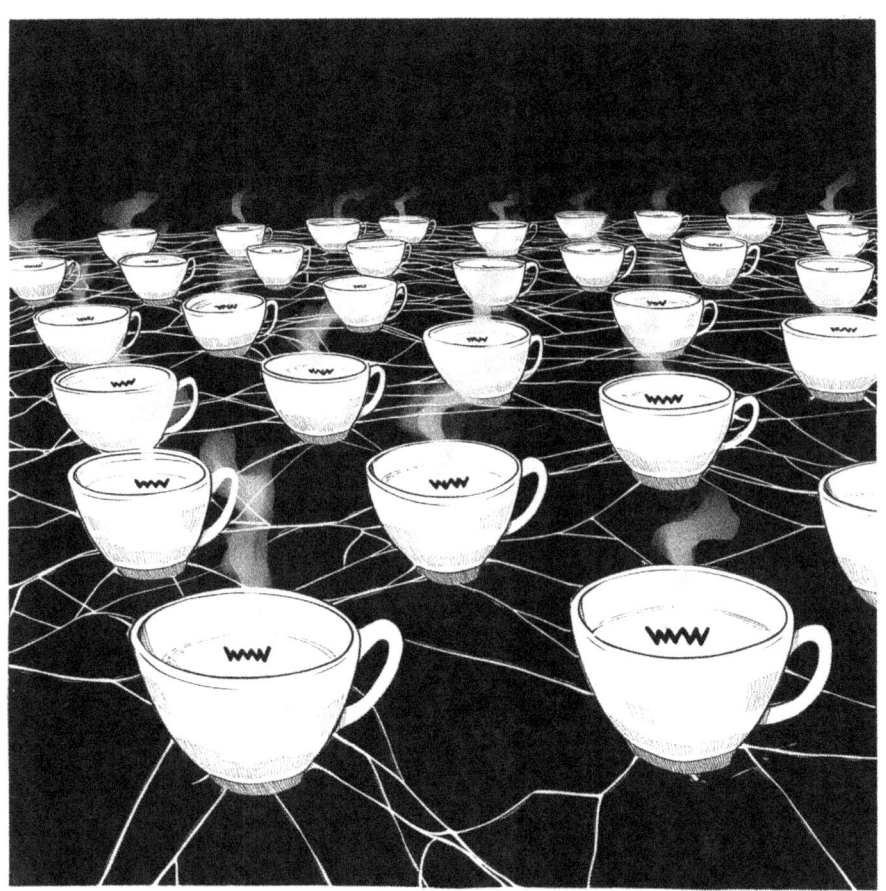

ALWAYS REMEMBER: THE MONEY FOR ONE LATTE CAN GET YOU ONE MORE DOMAIN.

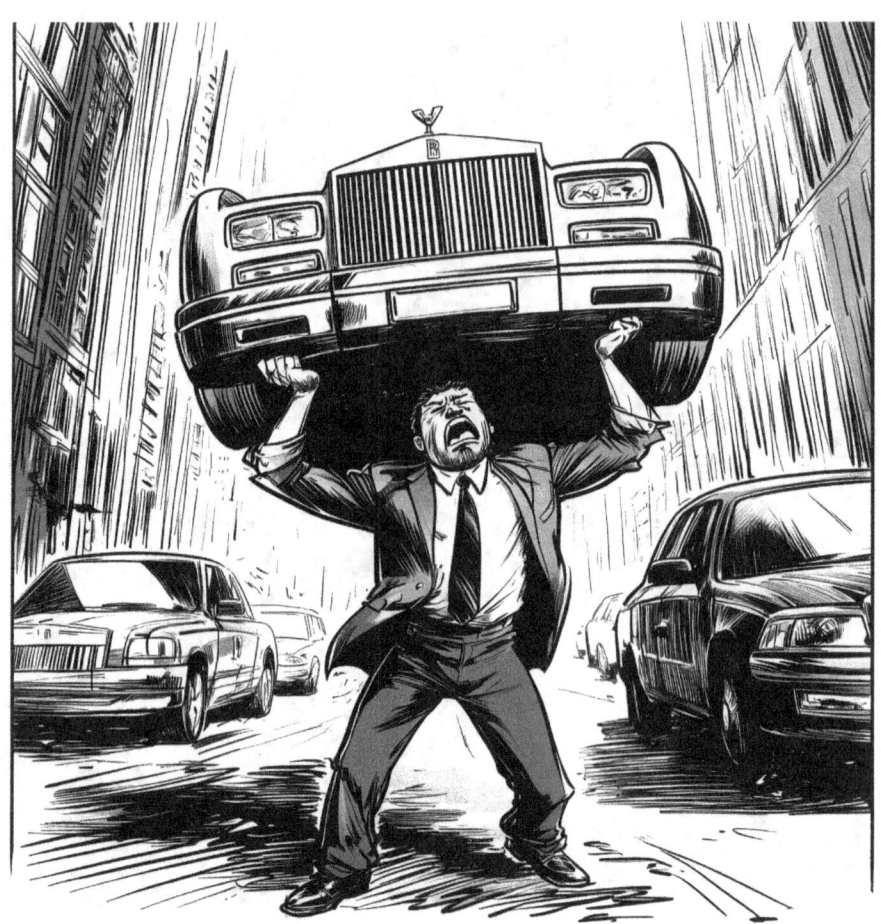

DON'T LOOK RICH.

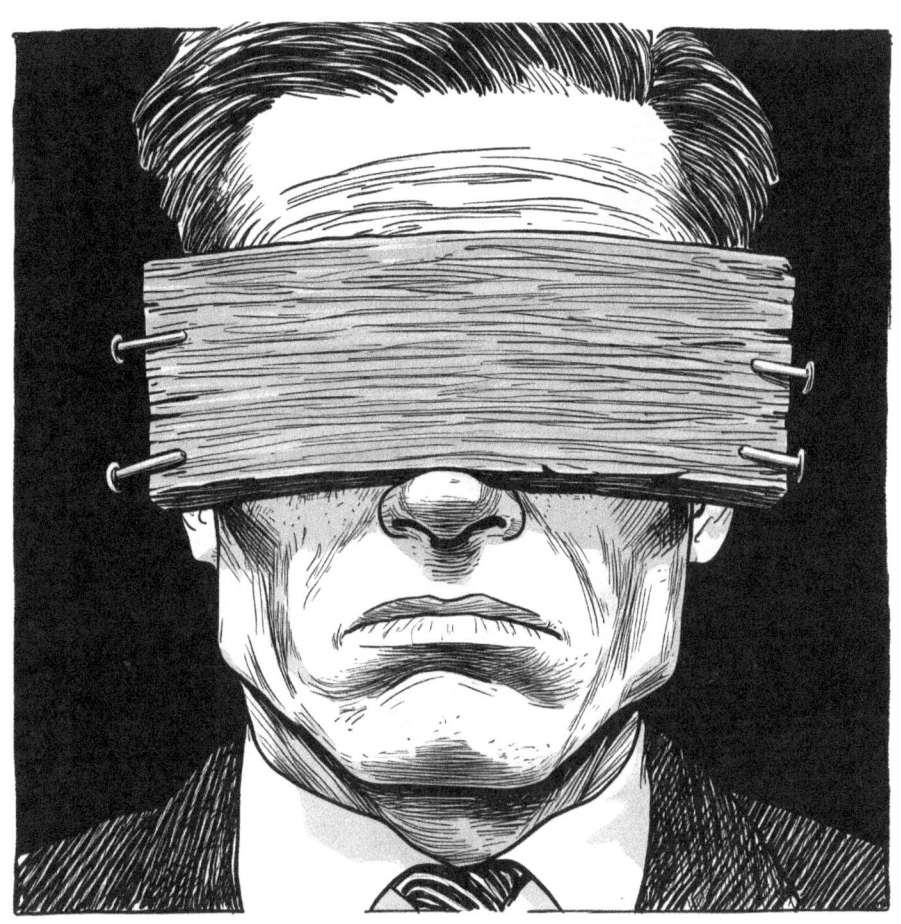

IF YOUR EYES SEE SOMEONE CLAIMING TO MAKE YOU RICH—CLOSE THEM.

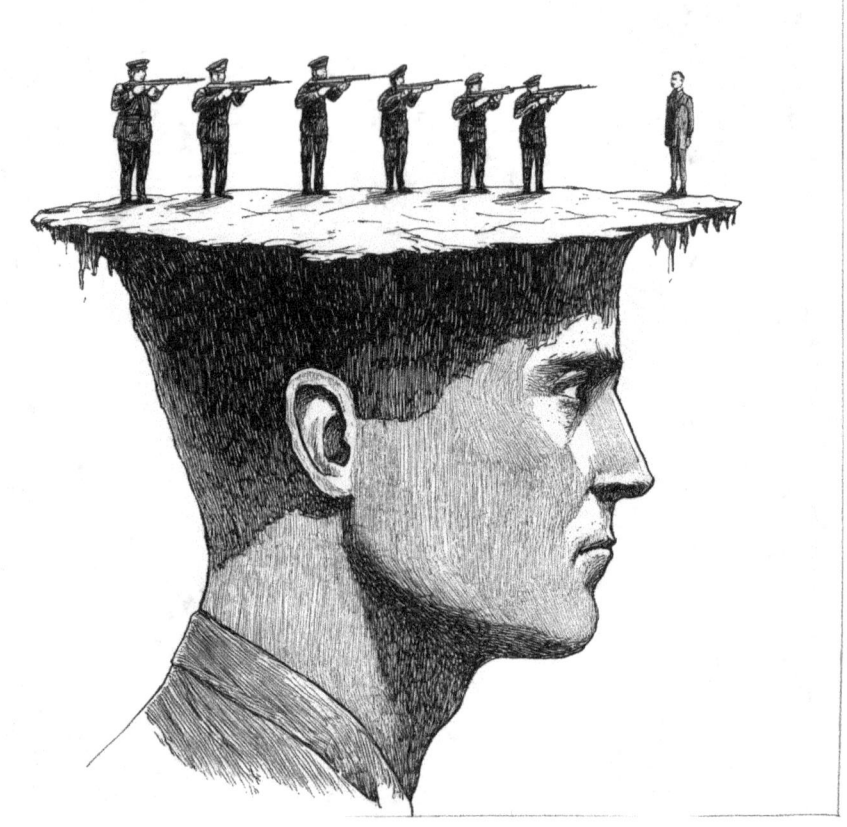

EXECUTE EXCUSES.

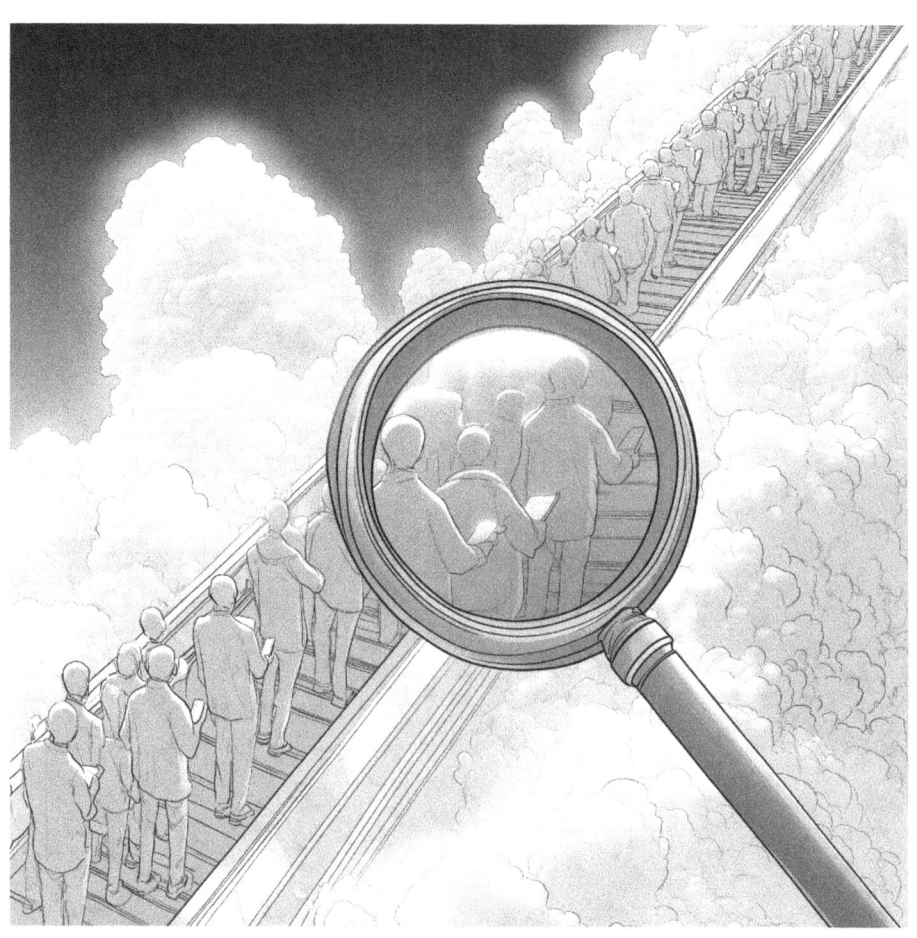

DON'T SCROLL.
SEARCH.

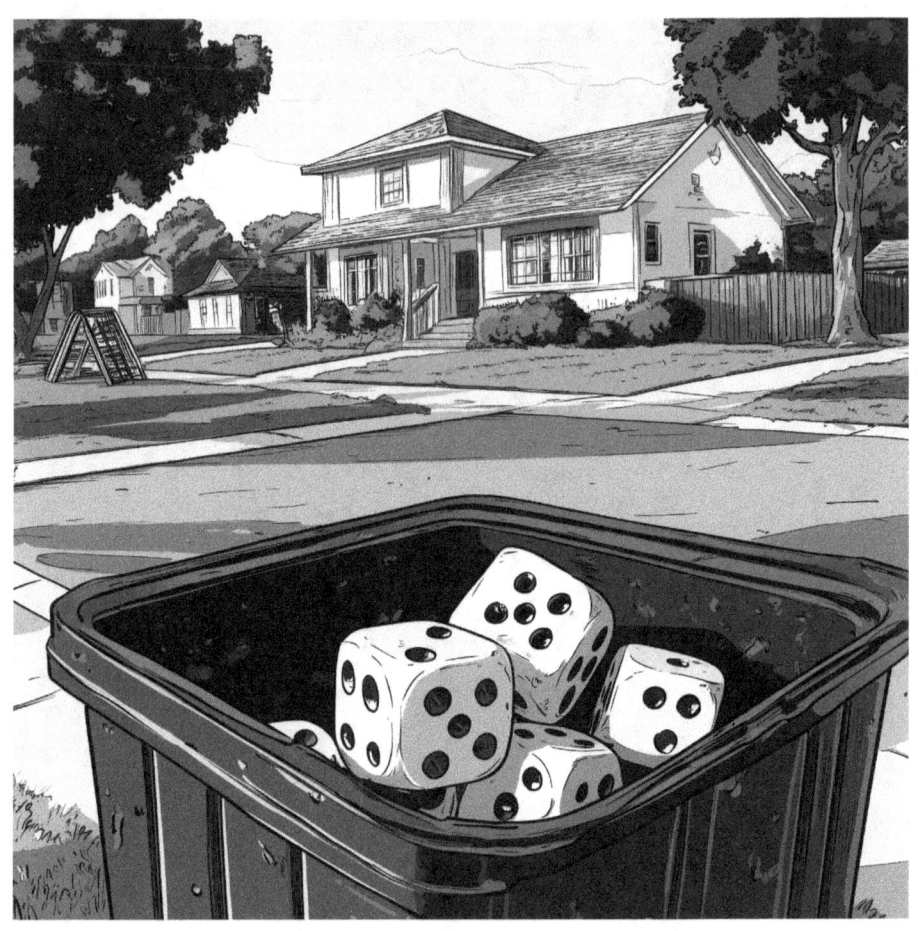

LOVE ASSETS. LEAVE BETS.

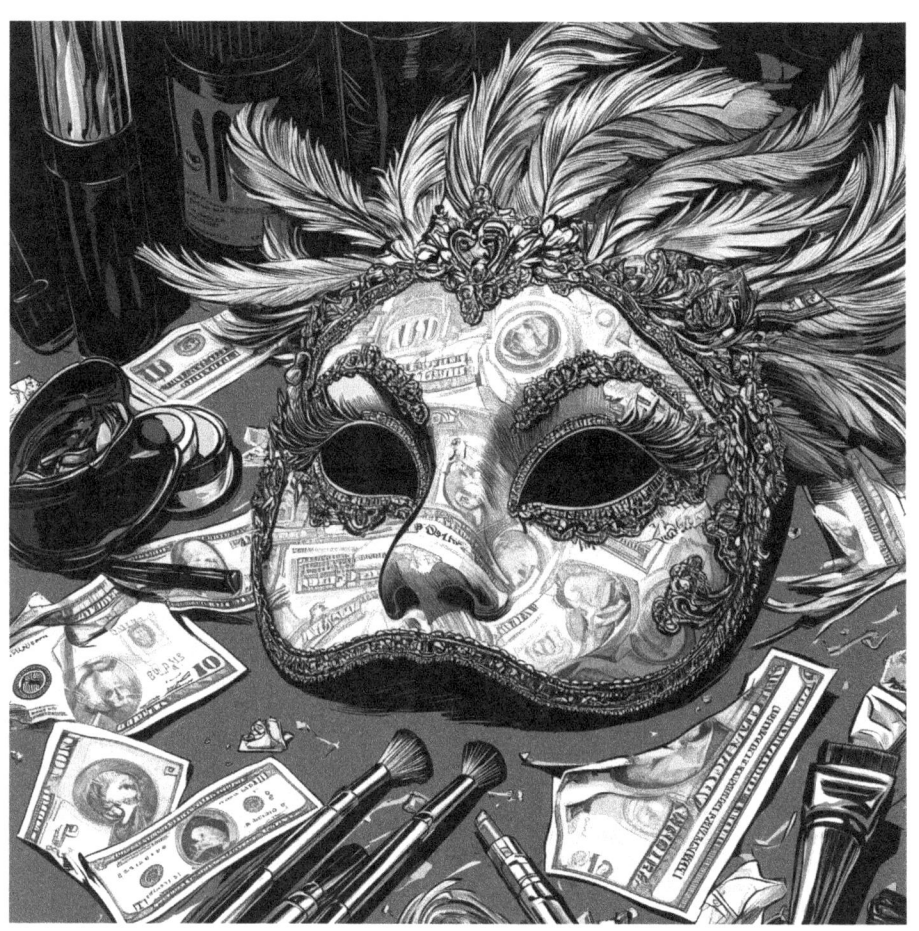

IF SELLOUT BRINGS PAYOUT – SELL OUT.

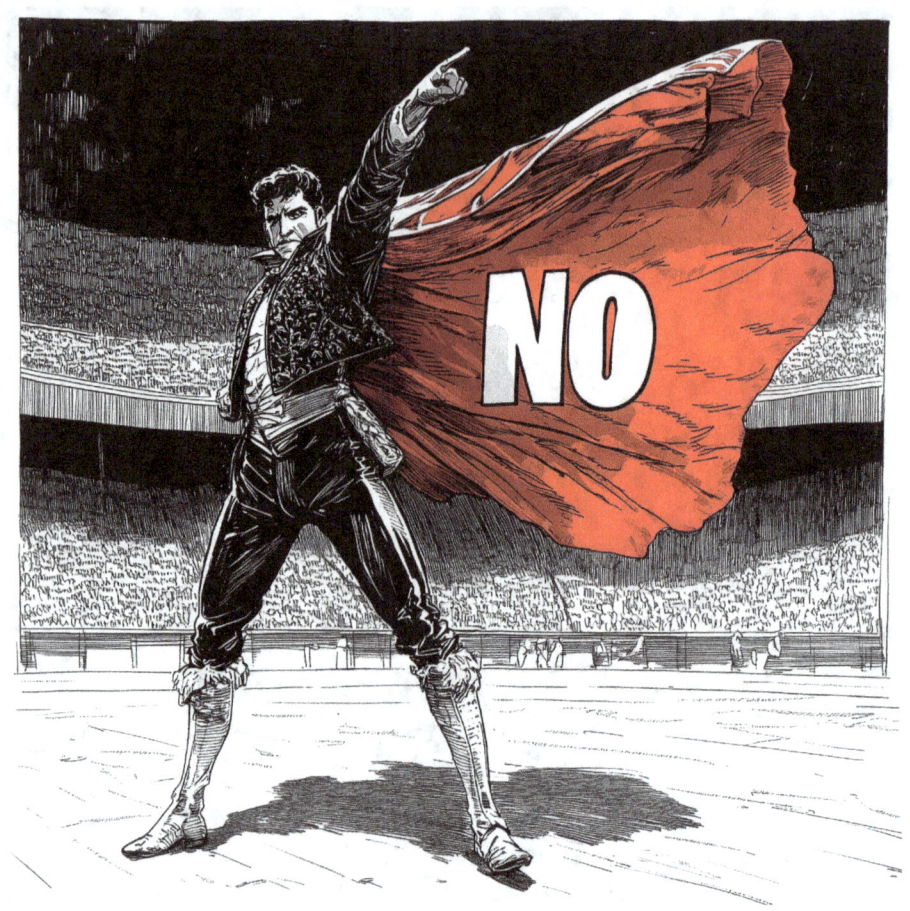

SAY NO FASTER.

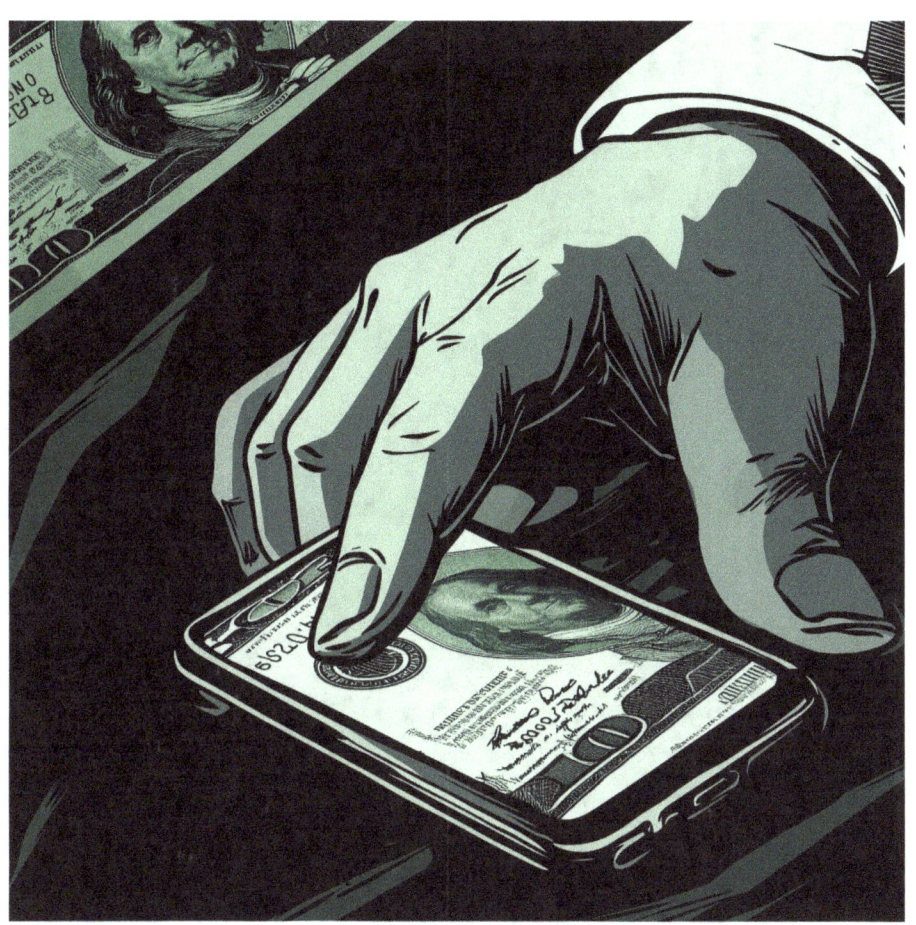

EVERY CLICK IS FOR MONEY.

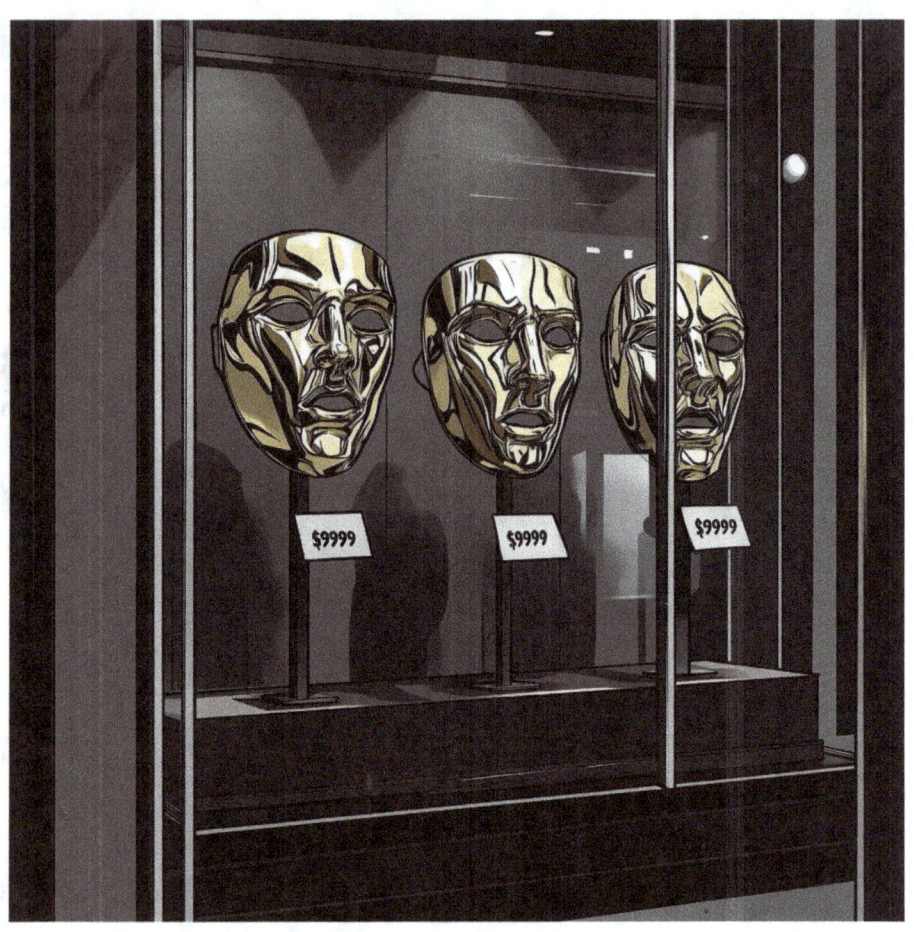

PUT A PRICE ON LAZINESS, IMPULSE, AND EGO—BEFORE YOU SPEND THEM.

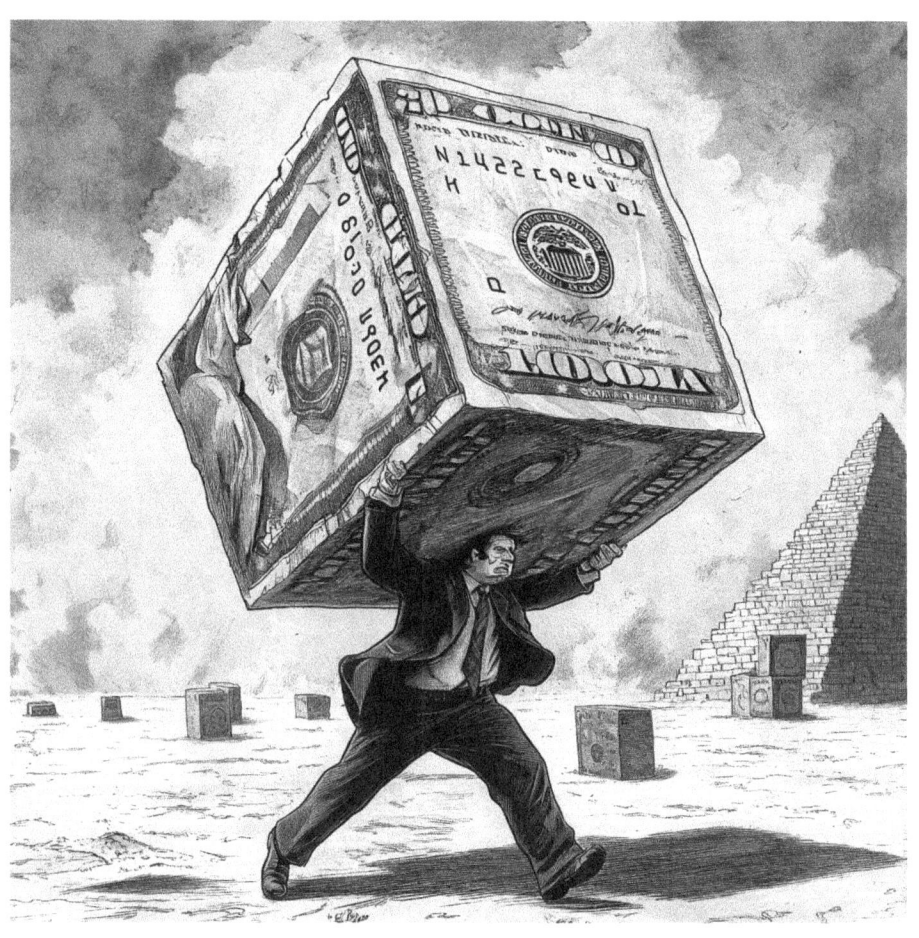

DO BORING BUT IMPORTANT TASKS.

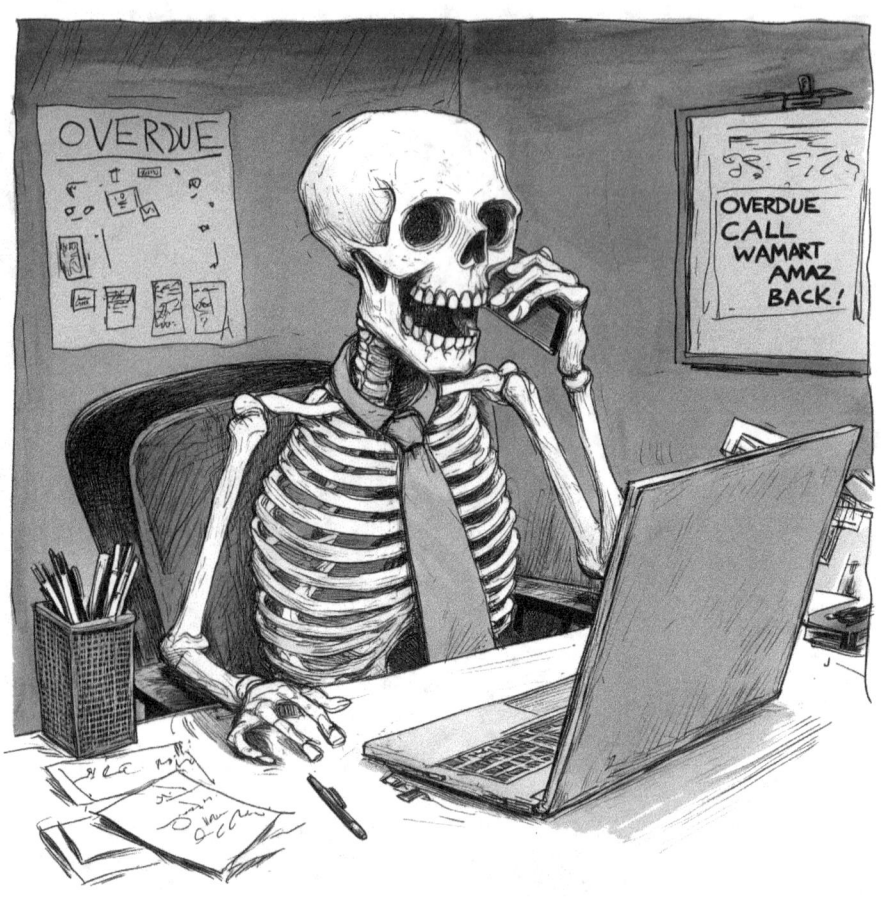

WORK LIKE YOU JUST CAME BACK FROM THE DEAD.

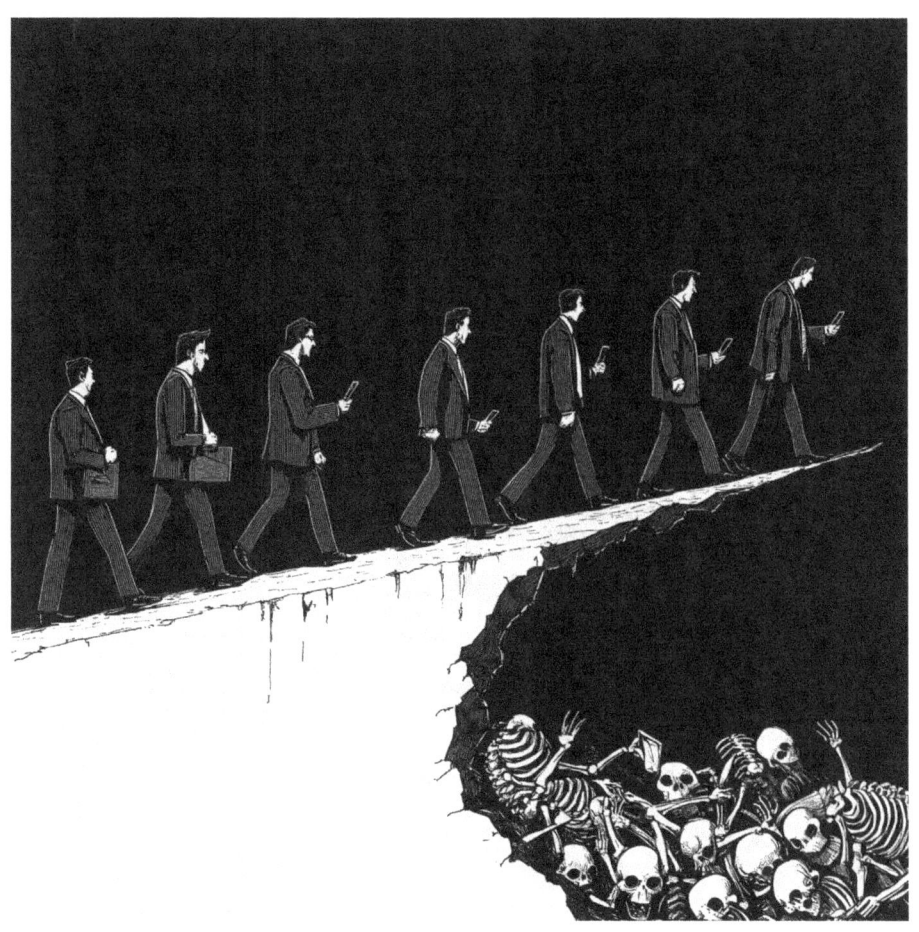

SKIPPING TRIAL AND ERROR IS THE REAL ERROR.

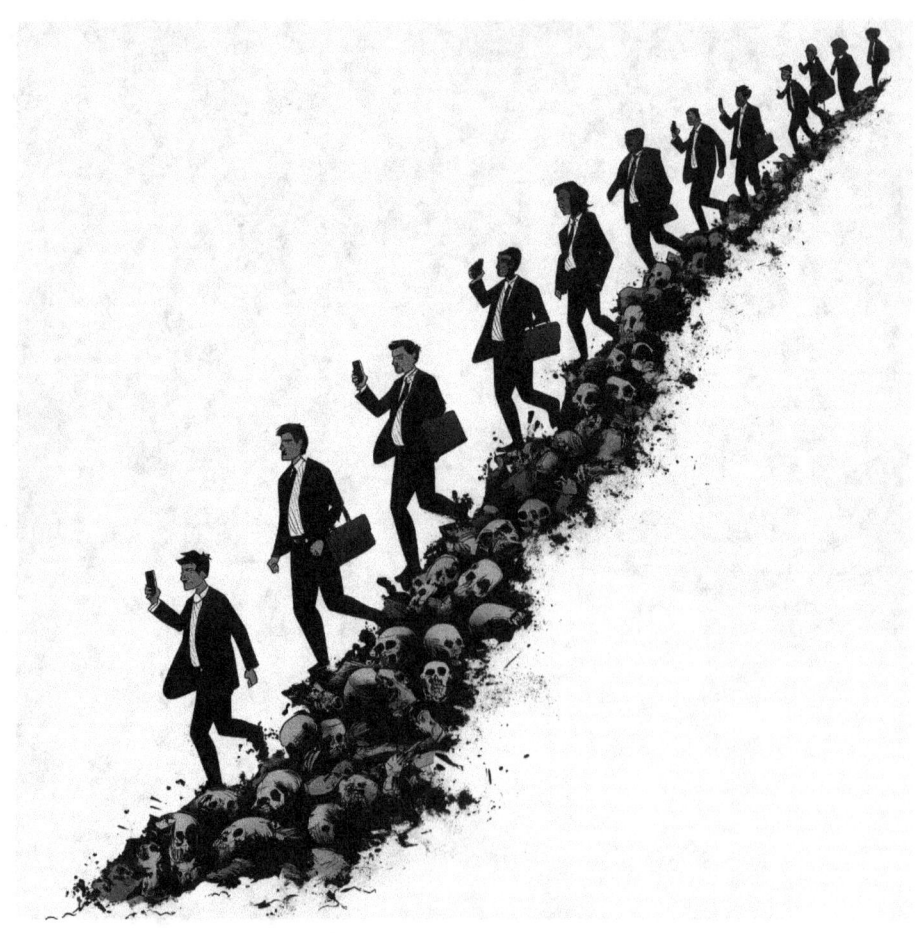

MISTAKES DON'T RUIN YOU. STAYING IN THEM DOES.

REAL MONEY ALWAYS CRAWLS IN.

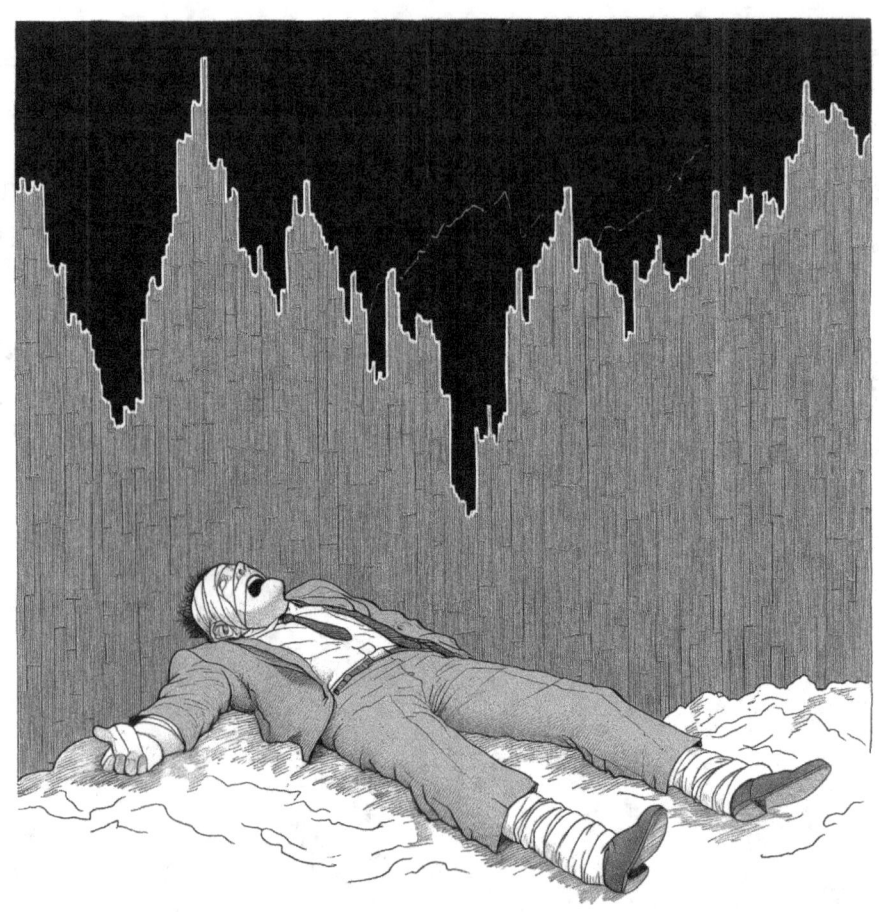

YOU MUST TRY TRADING STOCKS—JUST TO REALIZE HOW WRONG MOST OF YOUR INSTINCTS ARE. IT MIGHT BE THE MOST WORTHWHILE MONEY YOU'LL EVER SPEND.

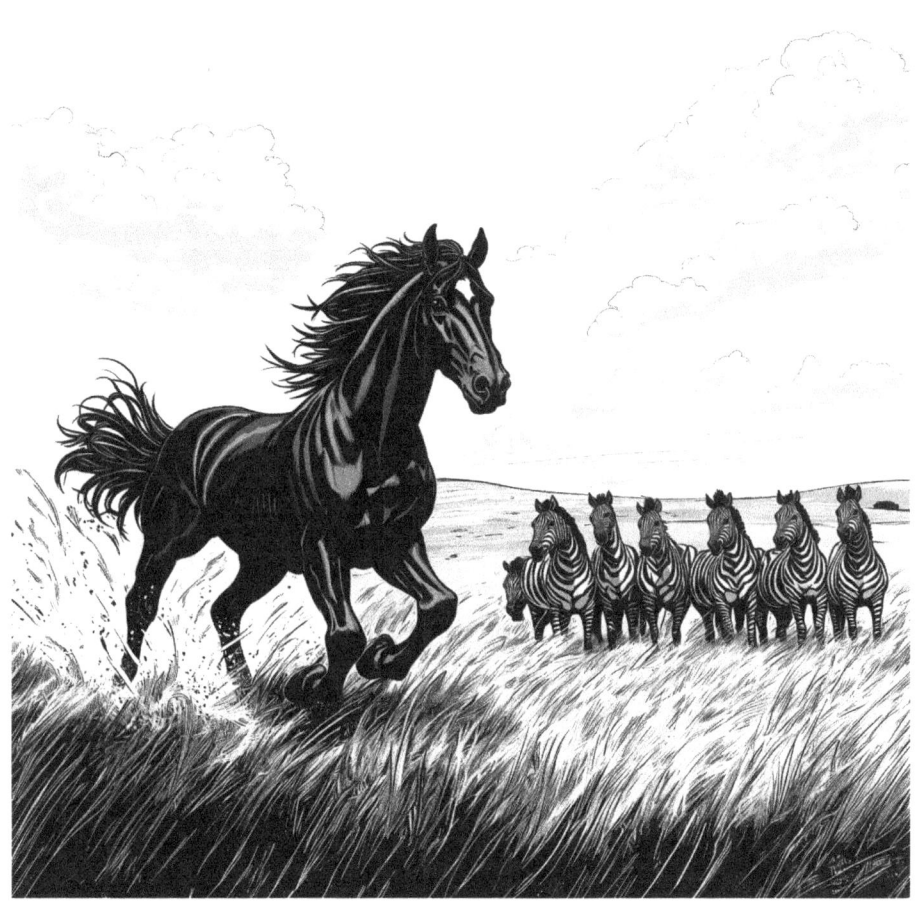

NEVER GO NEAR ANYONE IN A BIG LOGO COAT. NEVER BE ONE.

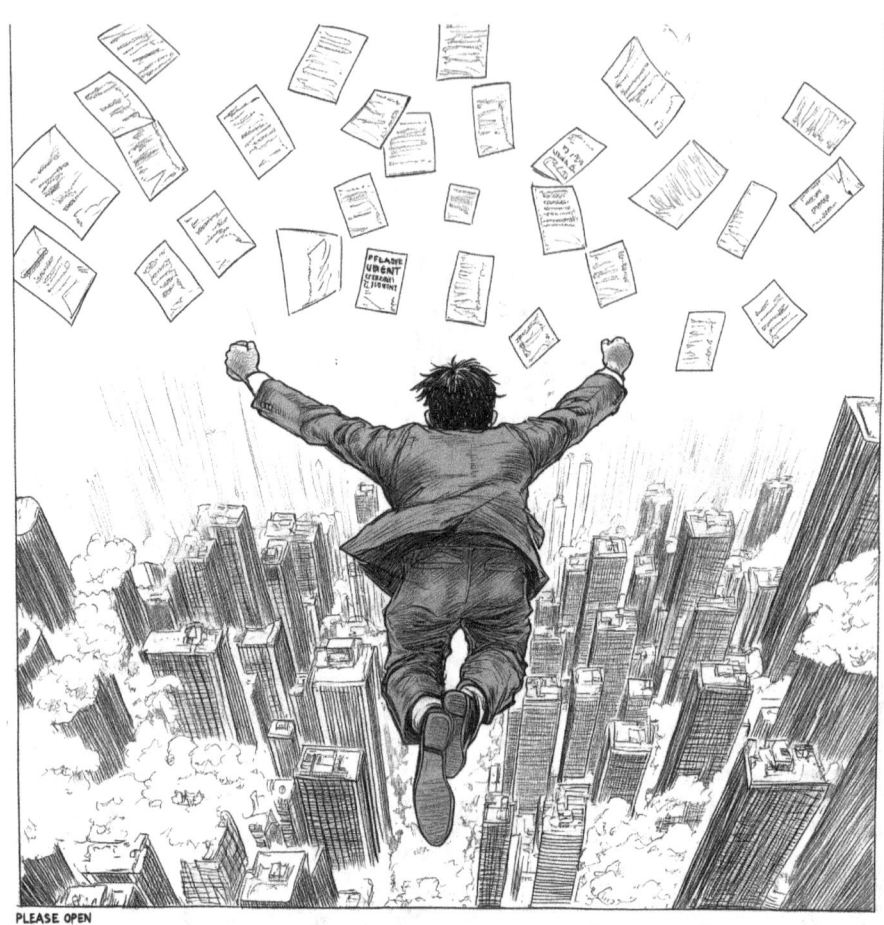

IF PROMOTING MAKES YOU SWEAT, KEEP SWEATING, KEEP PROMOTING.

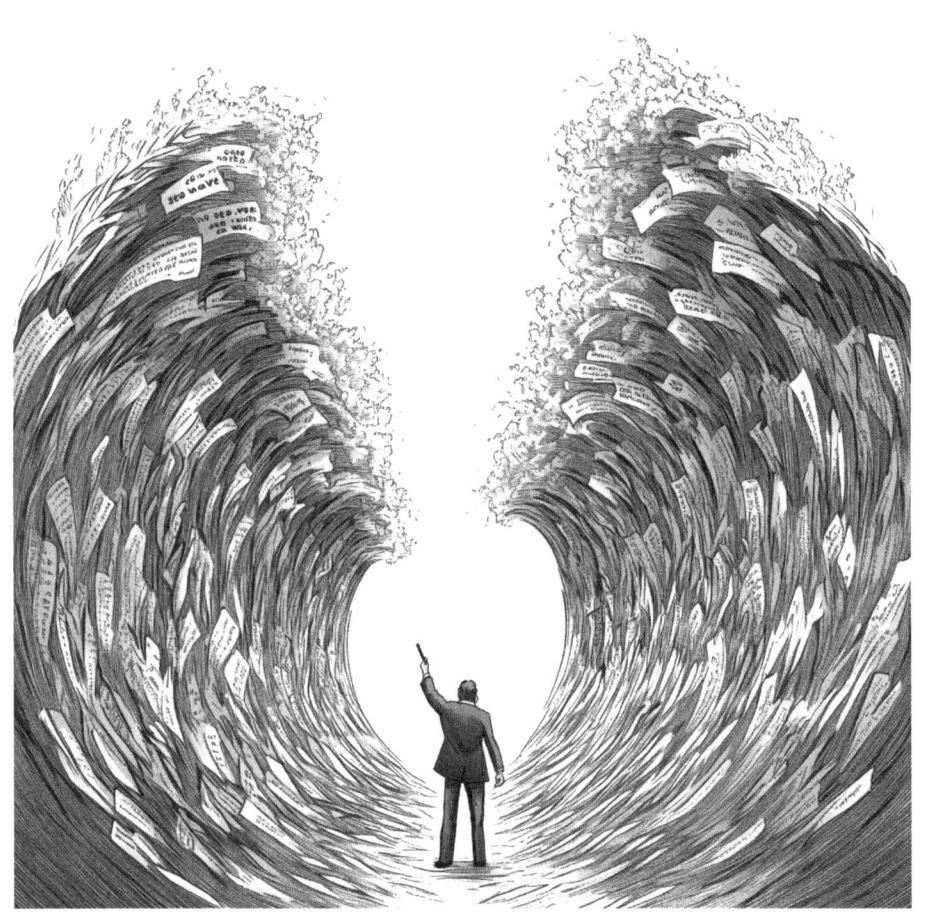

KEEP ANY PLAN UNDER 33 WORDS.

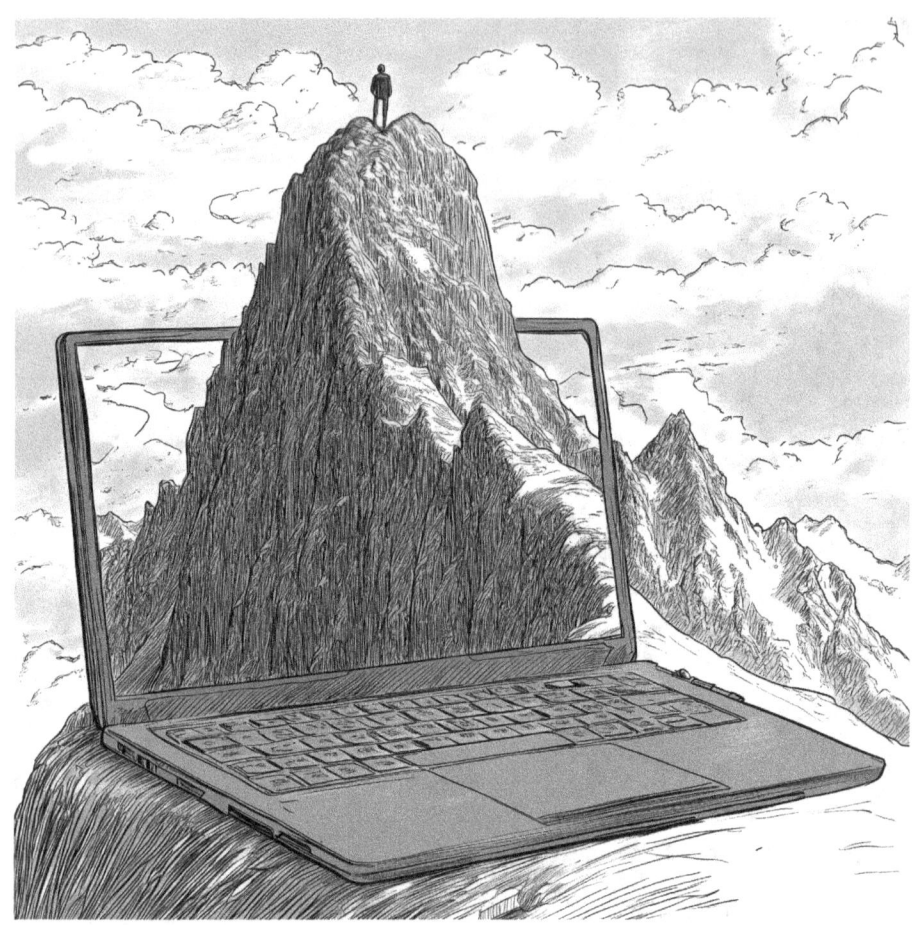

MAKE YOUR PASSWORD YOUR DREAM.

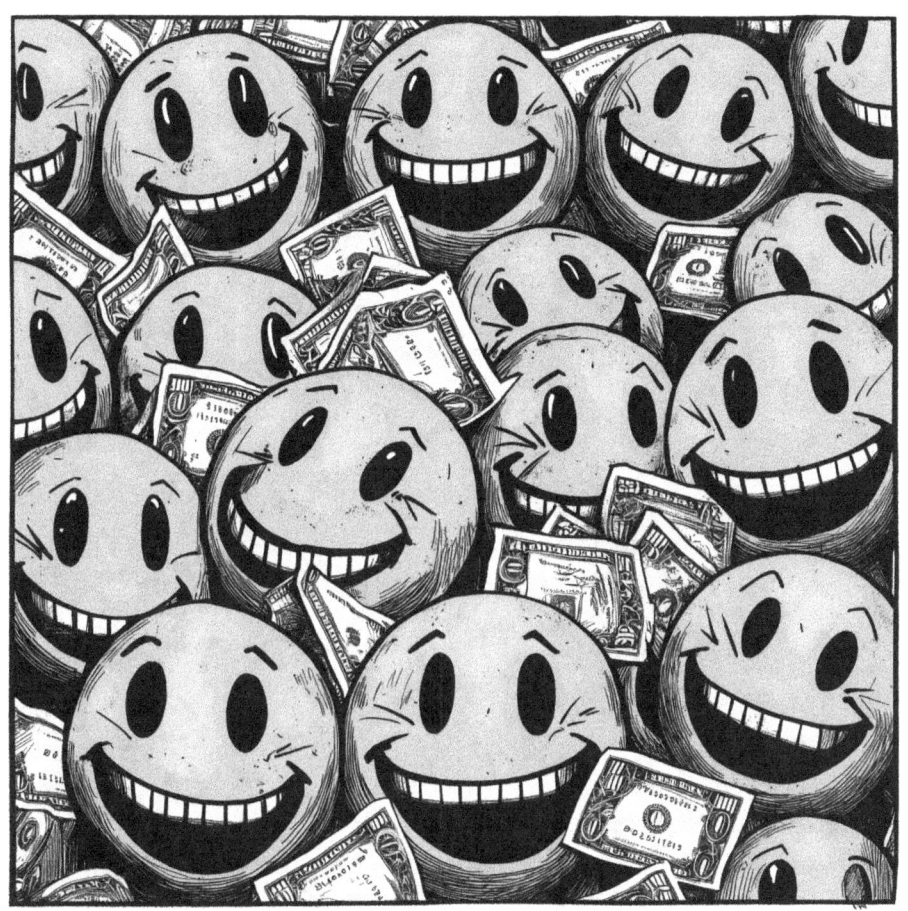

SMILE EVERY TIME YOU'RE REJECTED.

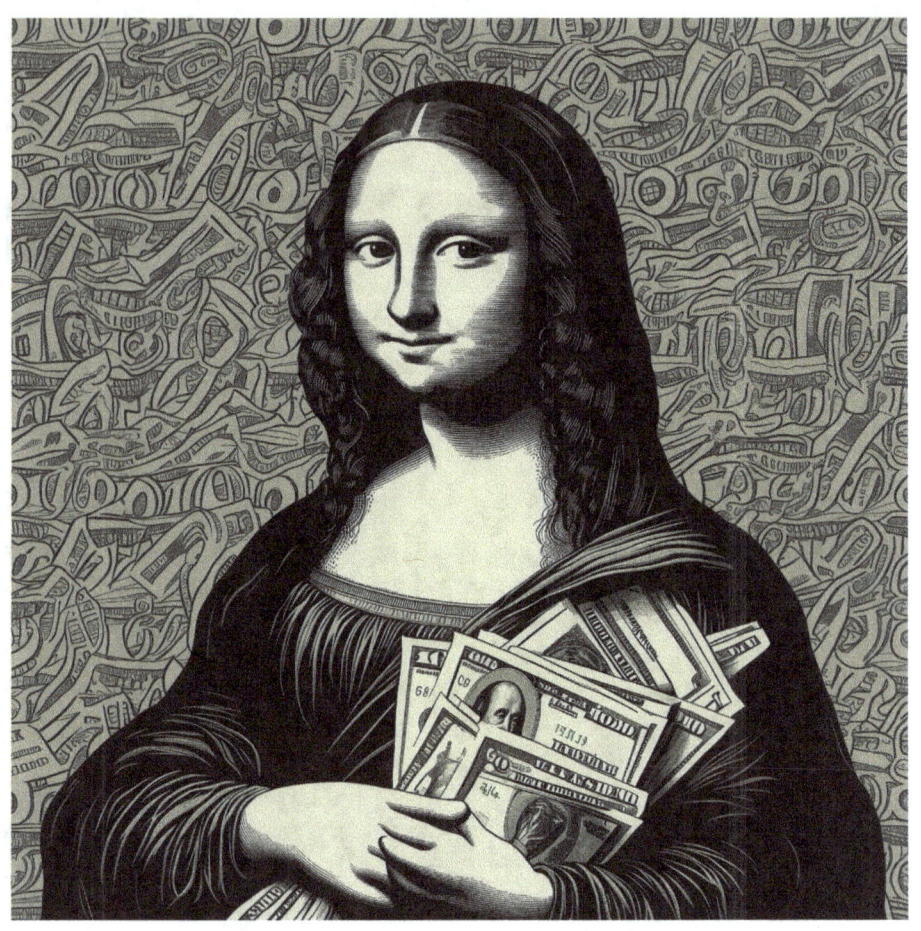

THE ONLY SUCCESS OF CREATION IS GETTING PAID.

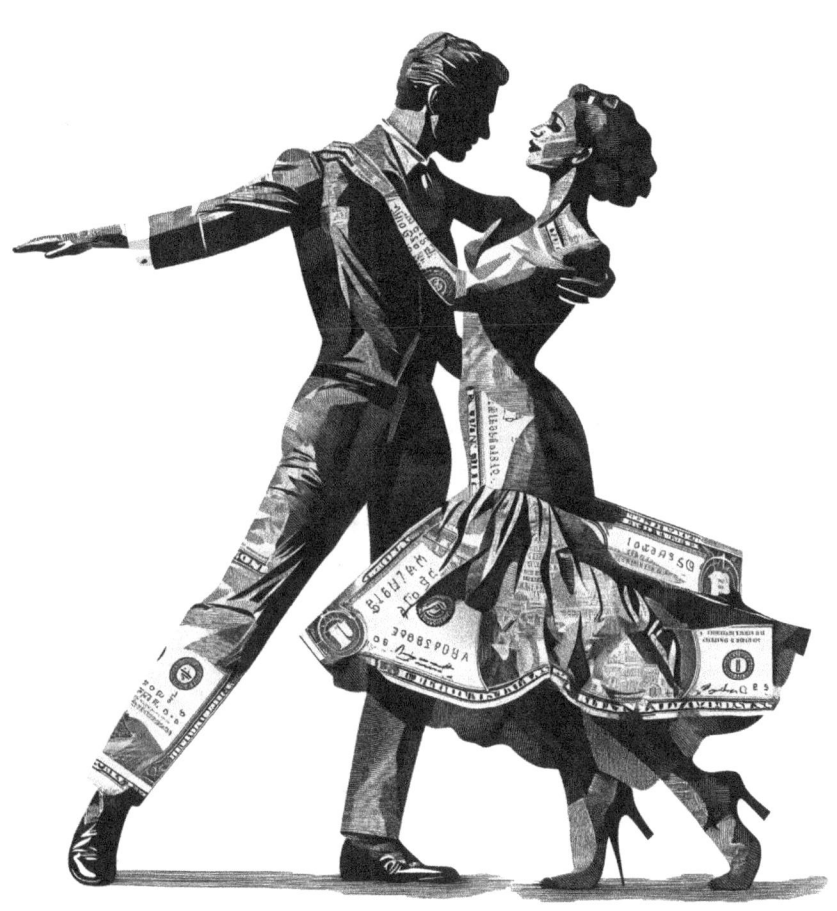

READ HUMAN NATURE TO REACH THE MONEY.

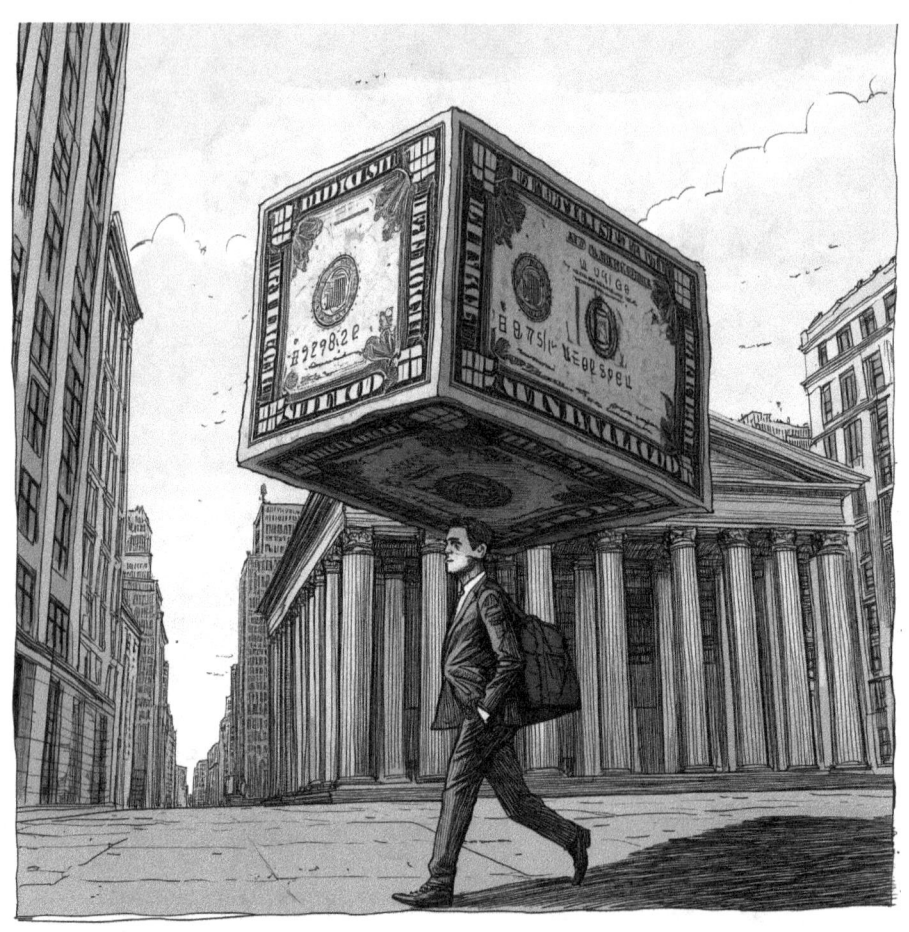

TECH GIANTS SURVIVE ON P/E ILLUSIONS, BANKS SURVIVE ONLY IF THERE'S NO BANK RUN—DARE TO BE SHAMELESS IN DEBT.

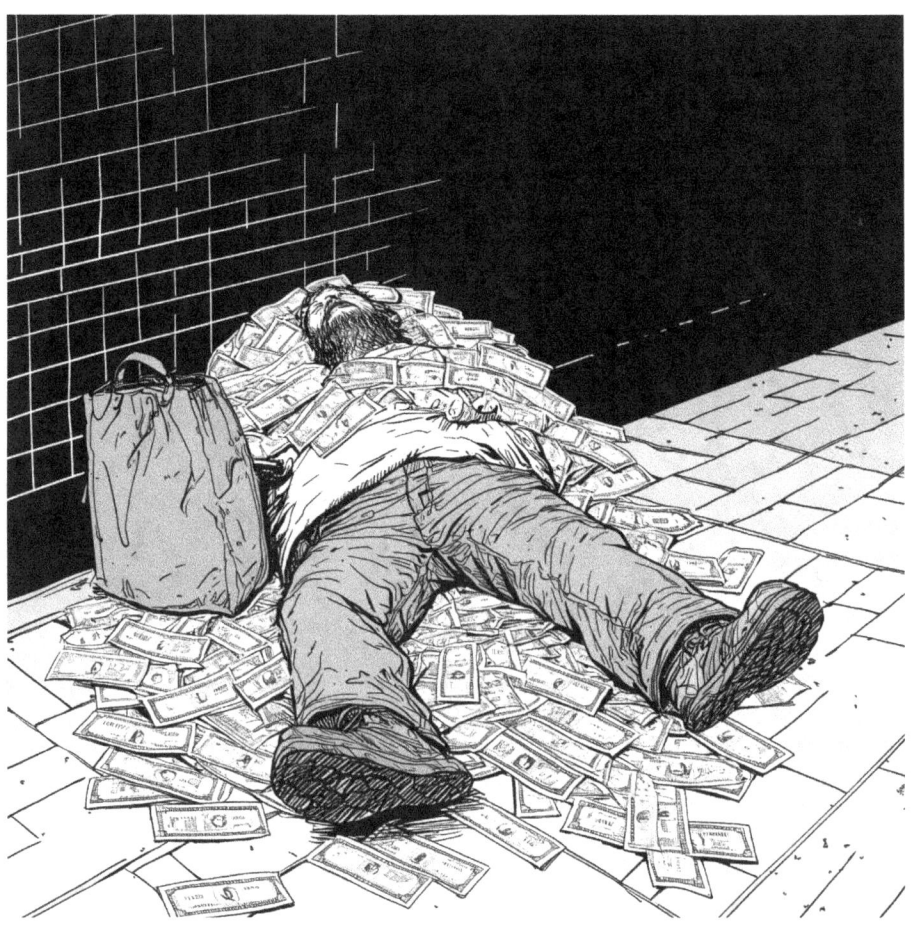

PREWRITE YOUR BANKRUPTCY COMEBACK PLAN.

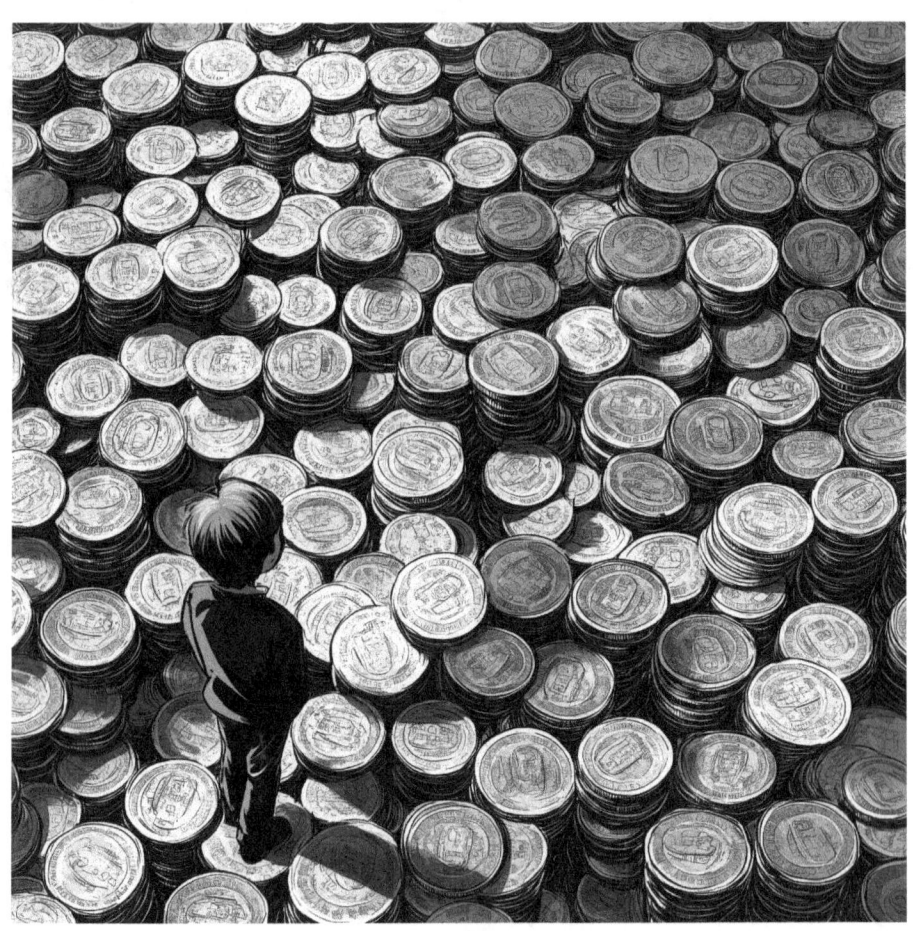

ALWAYS REMEMBER: 100 DOLLARS IS 10,000 CENTS.

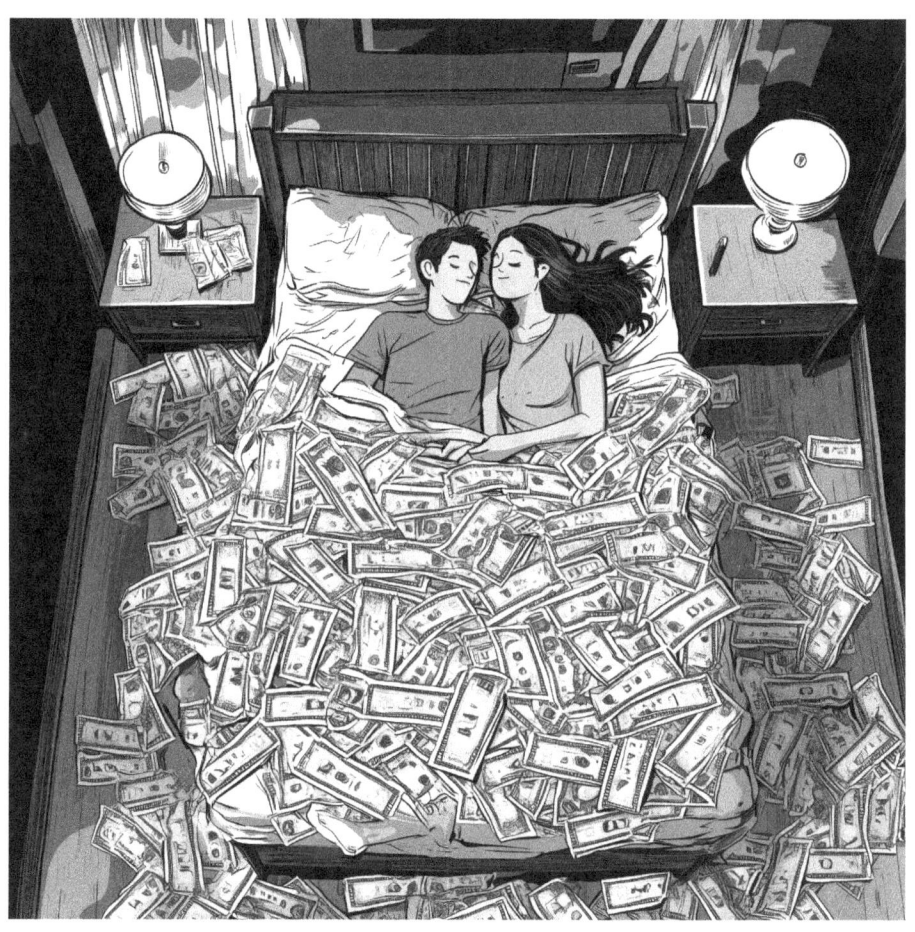

BLOW YOUR MONEY INTO YOUR OWN ACCOUNT.

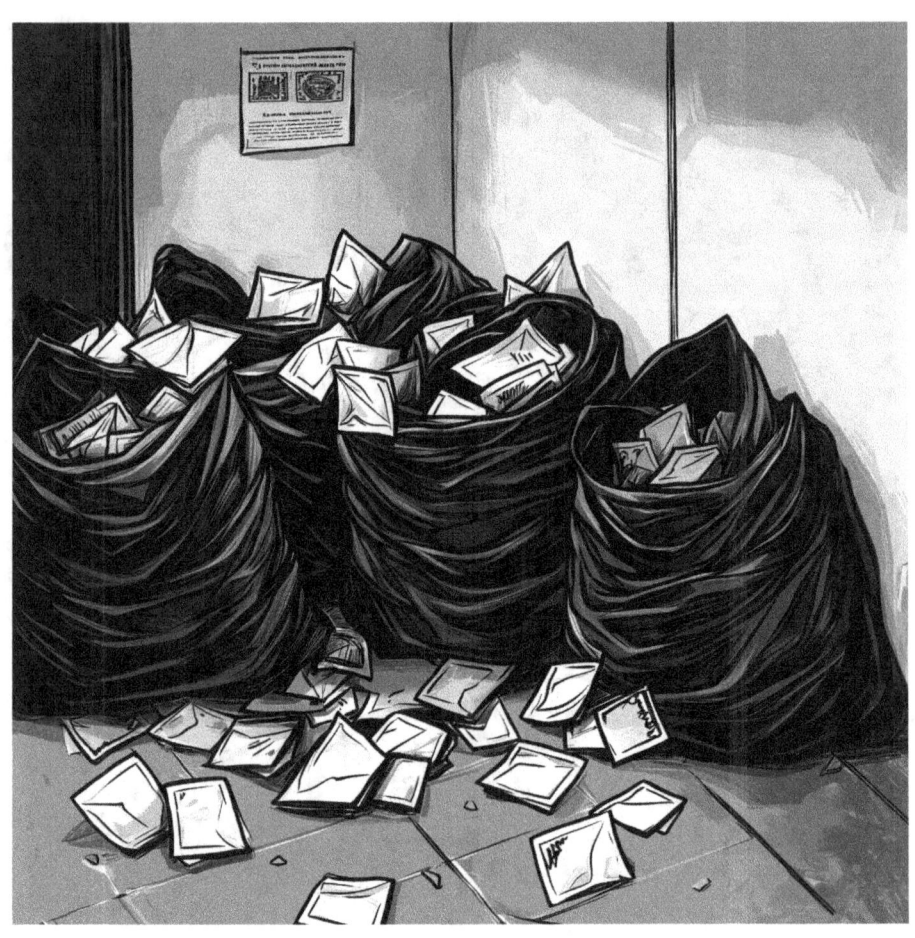

MARK EVERY NON-PROFITABLE EMAIL AS SPAM.

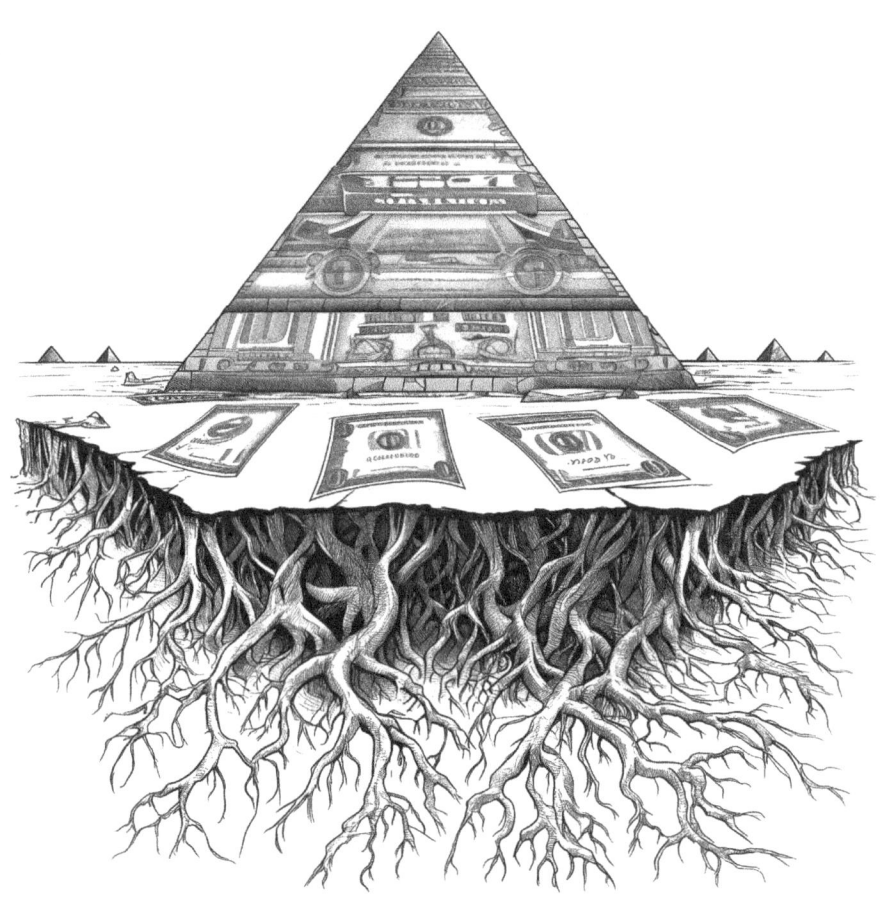

WEALTH GROWS LIKE A PLANT – SLOWLY, BY SINKING ROOTS. SPEED MEANS IT'S BEING UPROOTED.

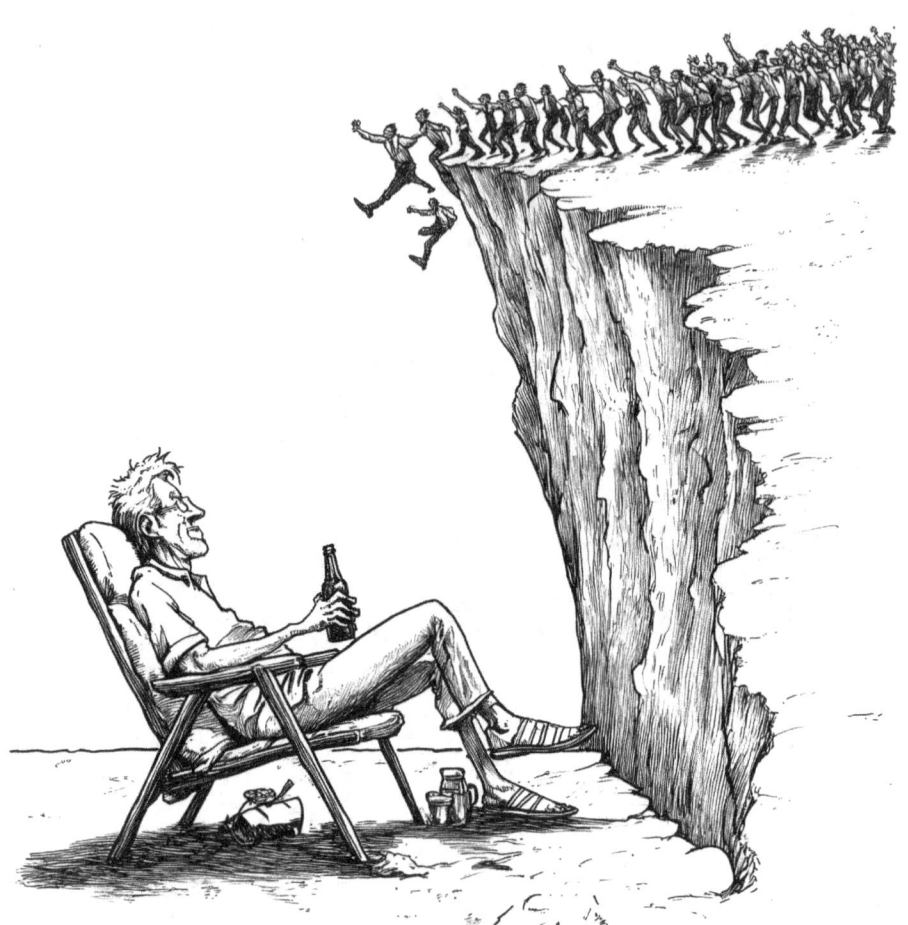

MORE IMPORTANT THAN DOING—IS NOT DOING.

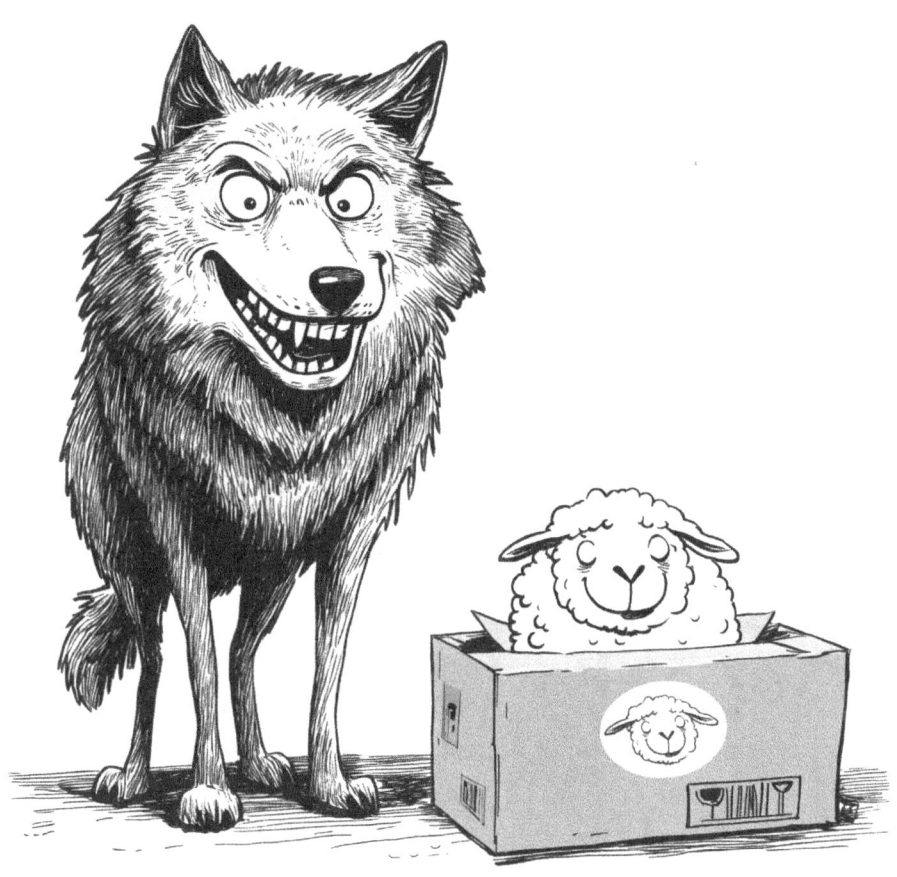

BE OBVIOUS. BE PAID.

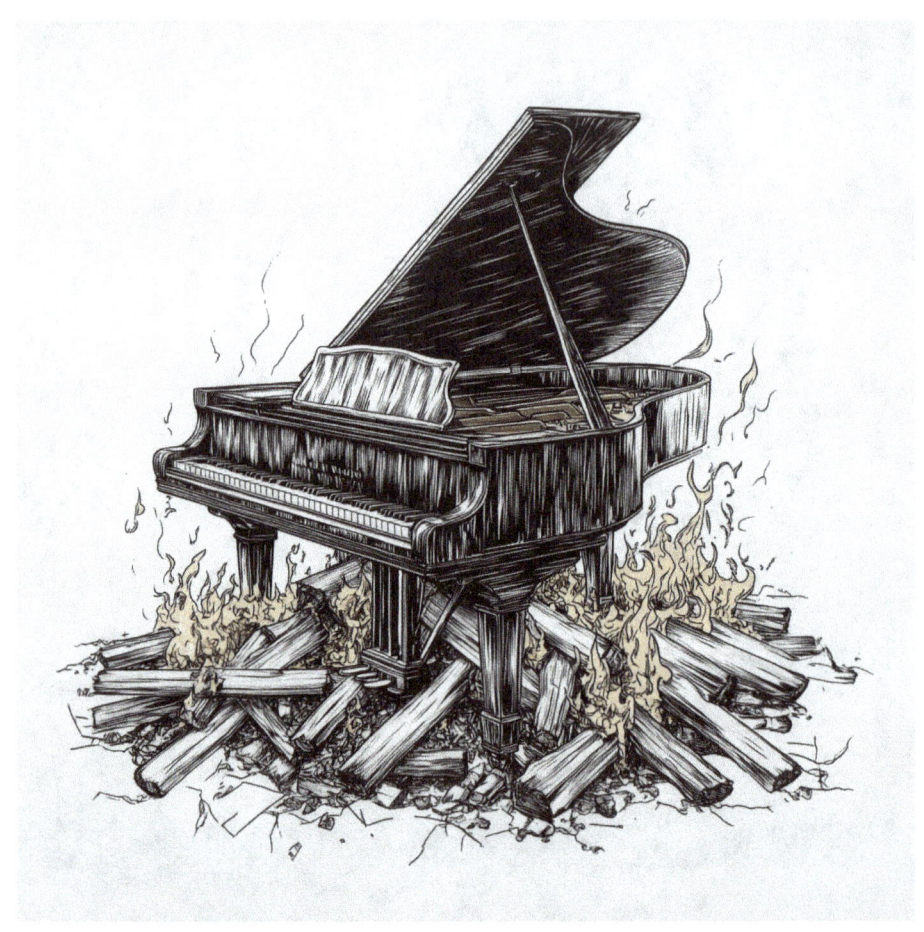

LET EVERY HOBBY THAT WON'T PAY DIE.

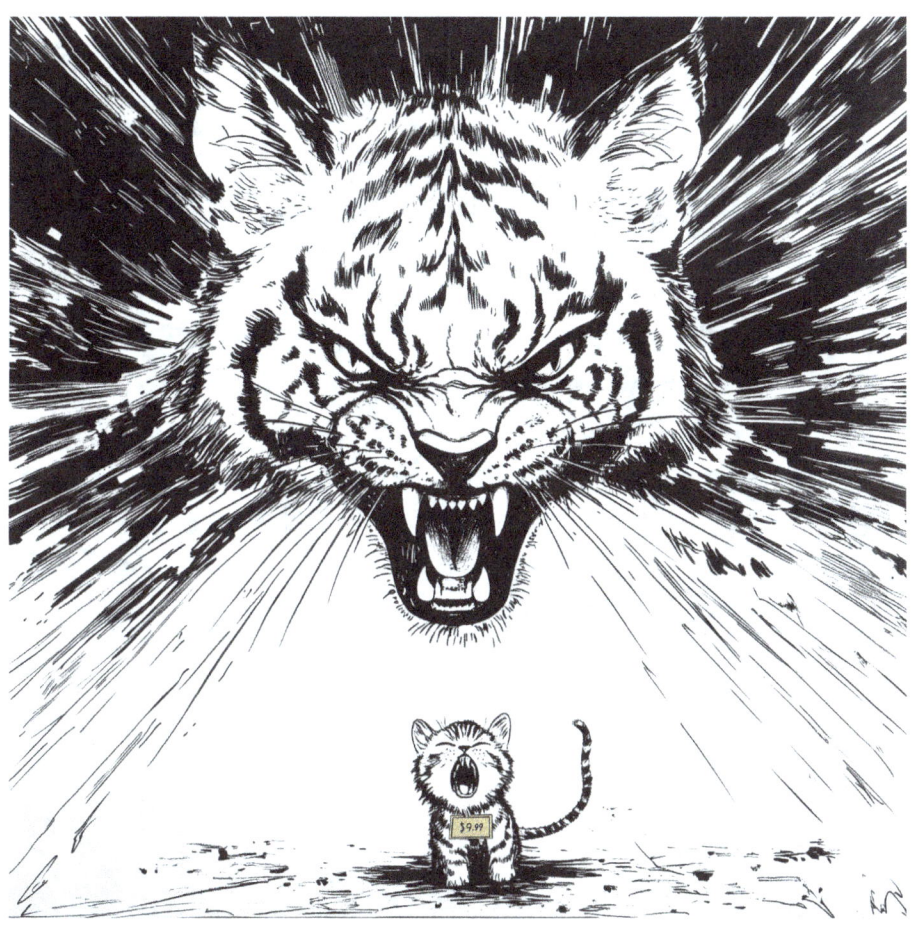

GET LOUDER WHEN YOU SELL.

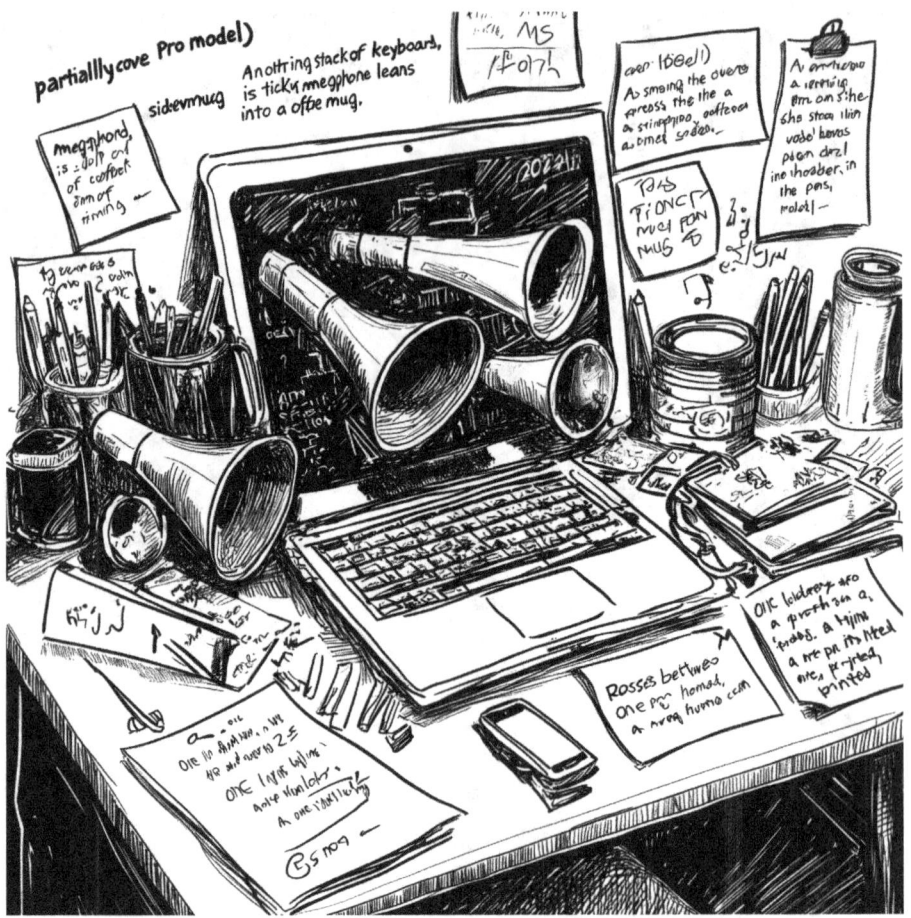

EVEN YOUR EMAIL SIGNATURE IS SELLING.

1957
Early Lanborghinii Product

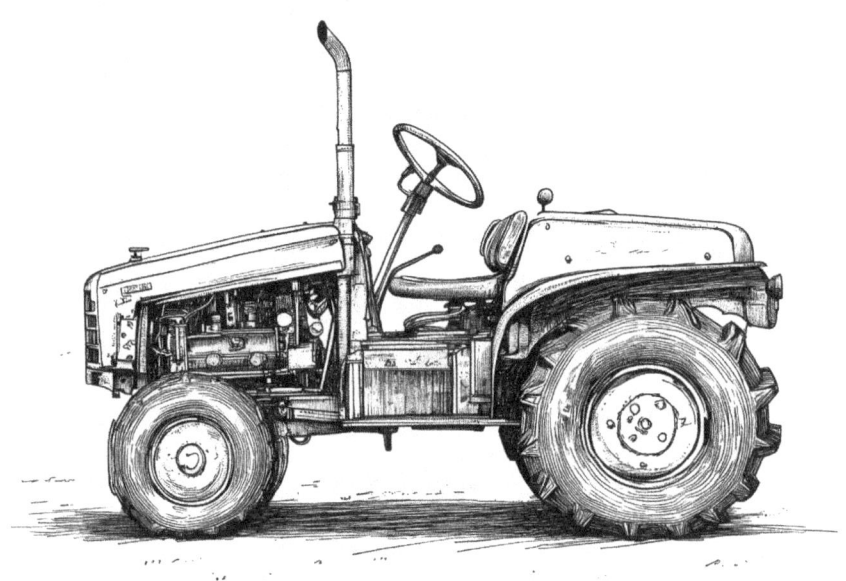

SELL IT BEFORE IT'S PERFECT.

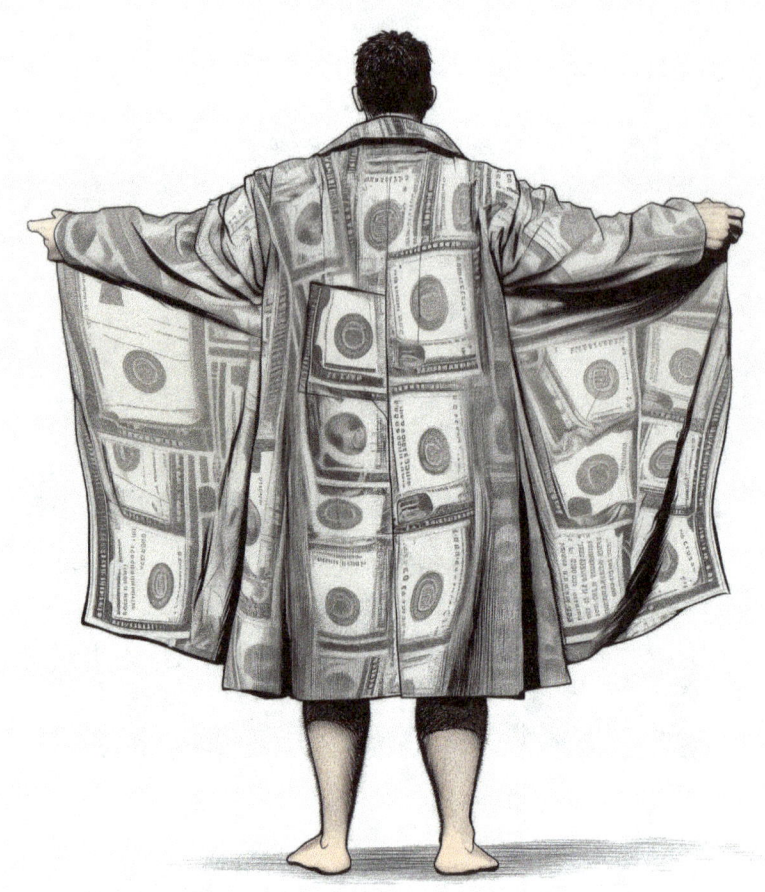

SHAMELESSLY SAY YOUR PRICE.

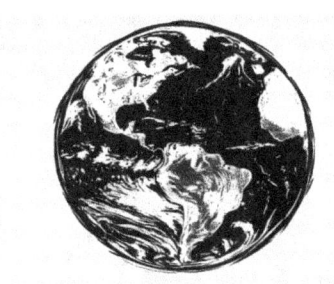

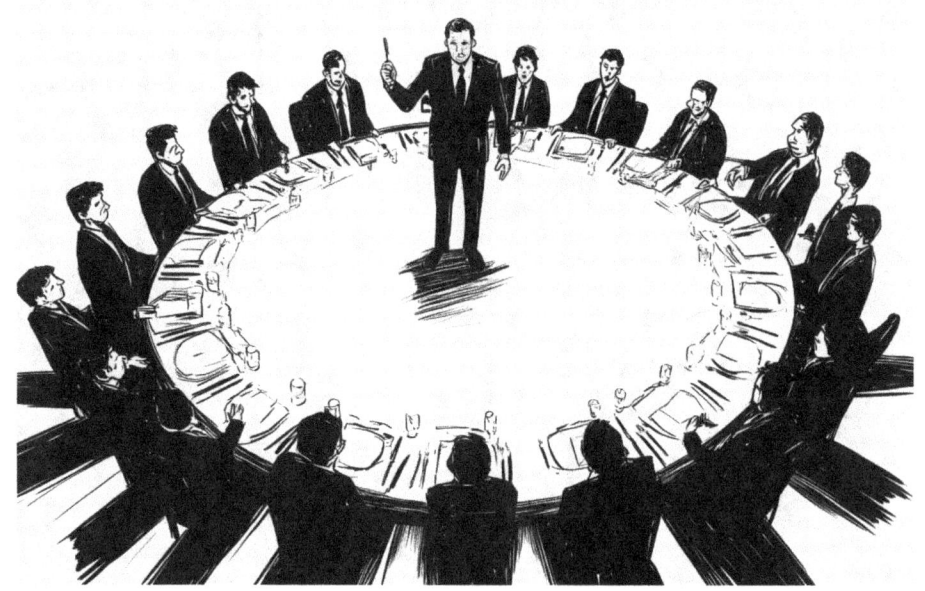

NOT THAT ANYONE ASKED – BUT HERE IT IS: YOU NEED TO EARN FROM THE MARKET. YOUR EMPLOYEES ONLY NEED TO EARN FROM YOU.

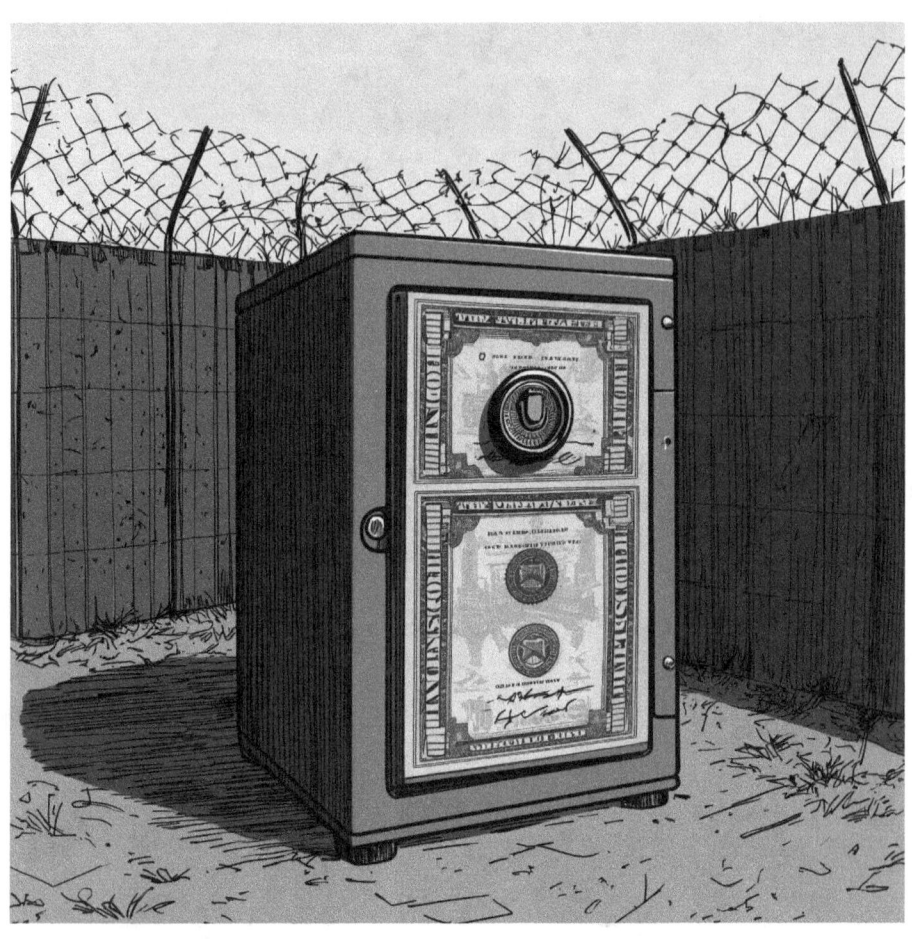

IF NOT SPENDING WON'T KILL YOU, OR SPENDING WON'T MAKE YOU IMMORTAL— DON'T DO IT.

STAY AWAY FROM ANYTHING THAT GUARANTEES OVERNIGHT WEALTH.

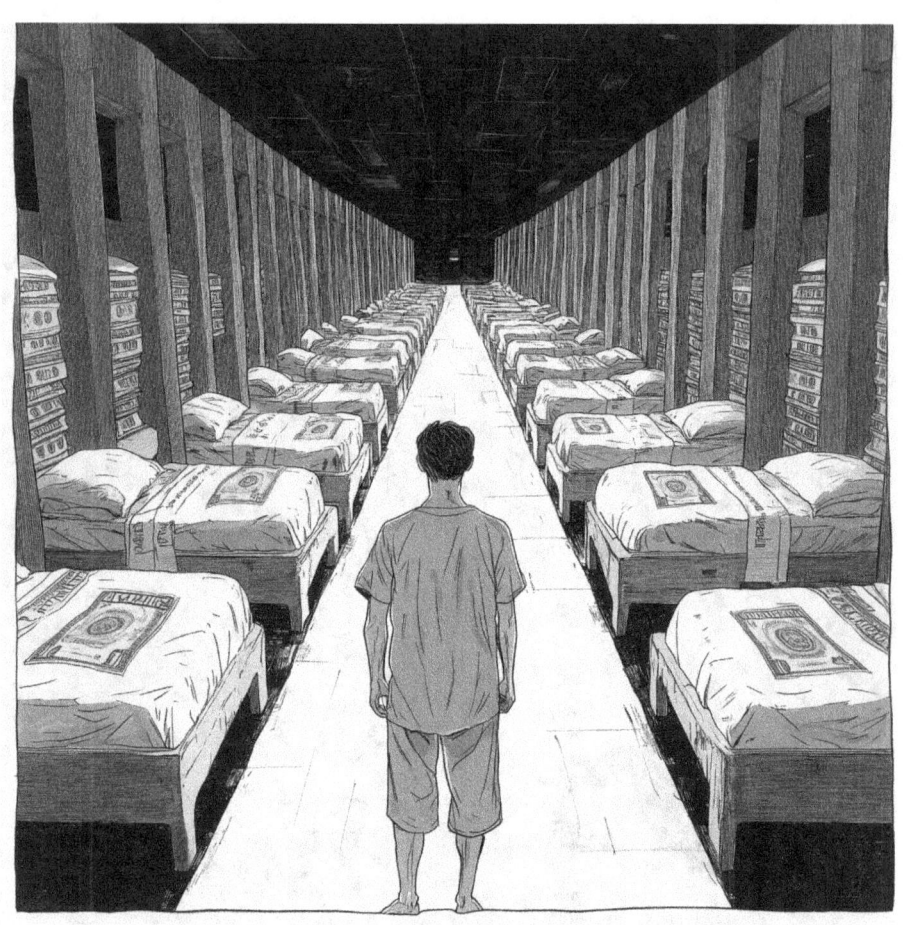

OPEN YOUR BANK ACCOUNTS BEFORE BED. SAY GOODNIGHT TO YOUR FAMILY—EVERY SINGLE DOLLAR.

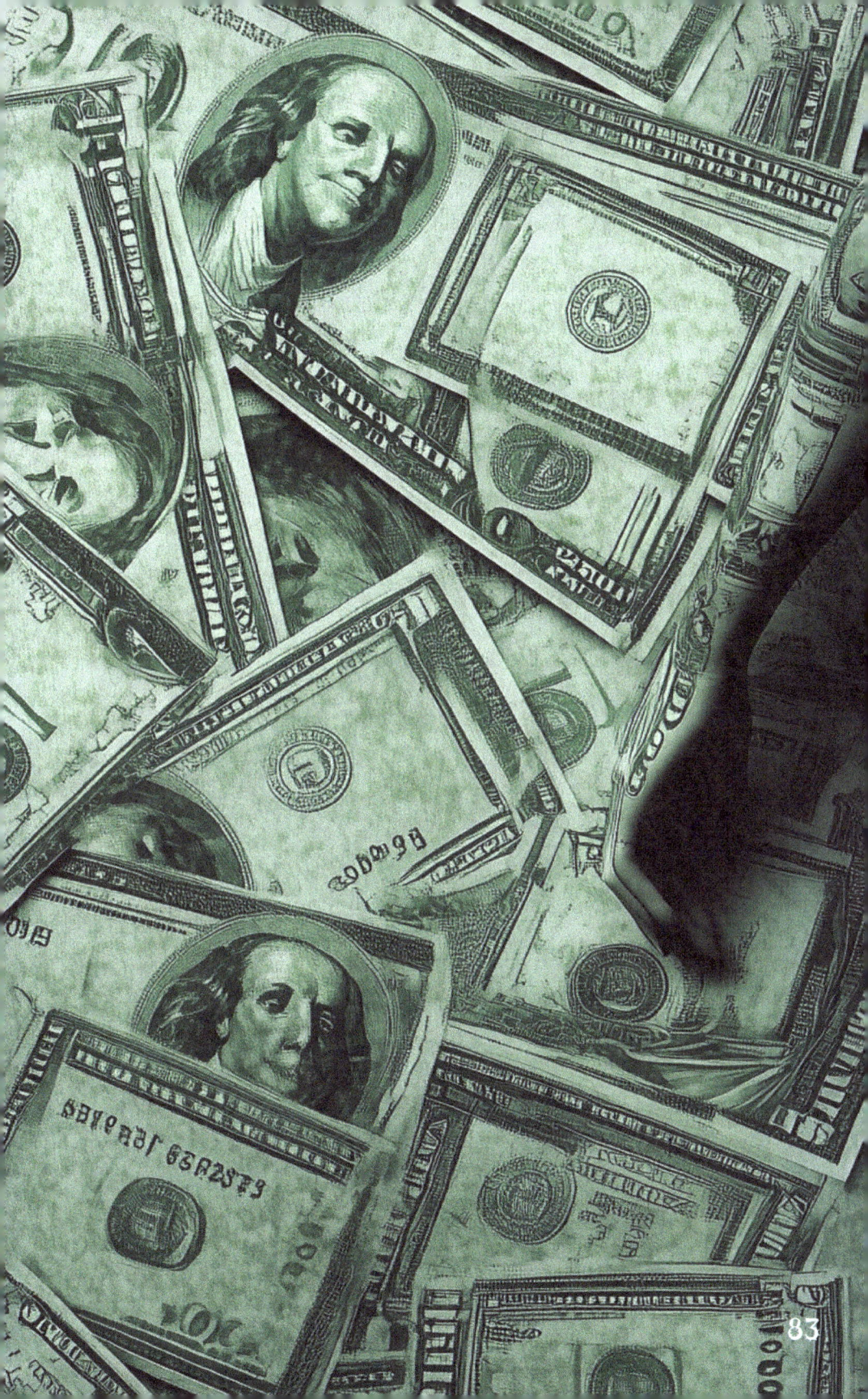

Read it word by word. Drill it again and again. Life's gonna test you on it!

Official Music Albums of This Book

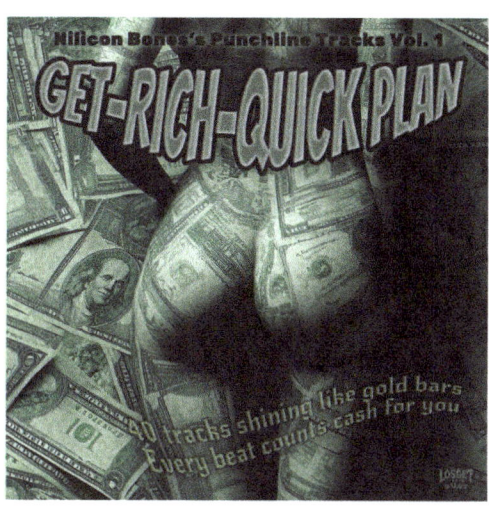

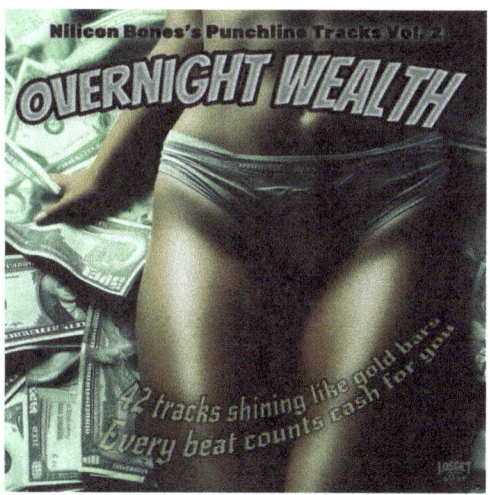

All 82 money rules in this book have been set to music, resulting in 82 original songs released as a two-album series across all major global music streaming platforms, including Spotify, Apple Music, Amazon Music, and YouTube Music.

Simply search for "Nilicon Bones" on your preferred platform to listen and explore.

LOSGET

Published in the United States by Losget Press,
Los Angeles.
Originally published in paperback in the United
States by Losget Press, in 2025.
Library of Congress Cataloging-in-Publication
Data
Names: Bones, Nilicon, author.
Title: *Nilicon Bones's Rich Punchlines & Illus-
trations Vol. 1: Trigger the Human High—And
Money Moans in Return* / all texts and illustra-
tions by the author.
Description: First edition. | Los Angeles: Losget
Press, 2025.
Identifiers: LCCN 2025908706 | ISBN 978-1-
951364-41-0
Subjects: LCSH: 1. Wealth—Quotations. 2. Suc-
cess—Quotations. 3. Graphic satire.
Classification: LCC PN6231.W38 2025 | DDC
332.024—dc23
First printed in the United States in 2025.
E-mail: losgetpress@gmail.com

www.ingramcontent.com/pod-product-compliance
Lightning Source LLC
Chambersburg PA
CBHW071219220526
45468CB00002B/666